S0-ARL-183

Lakewood Elementary School
6745 Hwy 79 N.
Buchanan, TN 38222

RED SON RISING

ADELE R. ARNOLD

DILLON PRESS, INC. ● MINNEAPOLIS, MINNESOTA

©1974 by Dillon Press, Inc. All rights reserved

Dillon Press, Inc., 500 South Third Street
Minneapolis, Minnesota 55415

Printed in the United States of America

Library of Congress Cataloging in Publication Data

Arnold, Adele R.
  Red son rising.

  SUMMARY: A biography of Apache Indian Carlos
Montezuma, who became a well-known physician.
  1. Montezuma, Carlos, 1866-1923 — Juvenile litera-
ture. [1. Montezuma, Carlos, 1866-1923.   2. Apache
Indians — Biography. 3. Indians of North America —
Biography.   4. Physicians]   I. Title.
E99.A6A75   610'.92'4 [B] [92]   74-17283
ISBN 0-87518-077-9

Contents

610
Arn

68

"The Eagle's Last Flight" by J. Roy Robertson: The face in this romantic portrait is a perfect likeness of Carlos Montezuma, the subject of this book, at the time he came to Chicago.

Preface

Among the Native Americans, few tribes were as warlike as the Apaches of the Southwest. When hunting was poor, they would raid neighboring tribes for the food they needed for survival. Apache raids continued even after the United States government took control of the Apache territory in 1848. The courage and ferocity of Apache warriors like Geronimo, Cochise, Victorio, and Mangas Coloradas is legendary.

This is the true story of a great Apache — but one whom fate decreed to be a *gentle* person, a servant of mankind. His story came from his own sharp memories of his boyhood and of his life as an adult, as well as from the records of other people. Some parts of his life remain a mystery, but from what is known it can be said that his is one of the greatest true-life adventure stories to come out of the Wild West.

Acknowledgments

Many persons helped in the research and documentation of this biography. First extensive study was done by the late Will C. Barnes, noted Arizona pioneer and author, and his widow generously shared his findings. Thanks also are due the late Frank C. Lockwood, Ph.D., of the University of Arizona faculty, who was the foremost authority on Apache Indians. Other helpers include the staff of the Phoenix Public Library, the Heard Museum of Indian Culture, and the Hayden Library at Arizona State University. My gratitude to all these sources is profound.

A.A.

CHAPTER 1

Home in the Wilderness

Dry autumn grass there on the apron of the mountain made a perfect hiding place. It was knee high, for the spring and summer of that year had brought many rains to make it grow. Late-summer drought had colored it tawny, matching the fur of the savage lions that roamed this wild Arizona area. Now it cradled a boy, who felt a wave of excitement race over him as he lay there listening.

"Something is coming!" He almost whispered the thought from sheer excitement.

The boy lay flat on his chest with his chin propped on a flat stone. In fact, he looked much like a stone himself, for he was naked and his skin was reddish brown, and he hadn't moved a muscle for a long while.

"It is not a lion," he told himself silently. "It hops."

The boy's eyelids were nearly shut. "Wild creatures have marvelous vision," Father had once told him. "They gaze into the eyes of their enemies, watching for movement. If you remain still and squint your eyes, you will appear harmless." The boy had found it to be true.

His hand held a string that he had woven of fibers from a wild plant. It too was tan and was hard to see in the dry grass. The string extended away from him about thirty steps, and was tied to a stick as long as a boy's forearm. The stick stood on end and held up a heavy flat rock, forming a tiny lean-to. Under the rock were a wild onion and some fresh watercress.

Still motionless, the boy watched for another long moment. Then he jerked his string.

Squee-e-e, squee-e-e, squee-e-e!

A shrill squeal of terror rang out, and the heavy rock began thumping against the earth. With the first sound, the boy leaped to his feet. He sped to the rock, reached under it, and grabbed two furry hind legs that were kicking furiously. In the same quick motion he swung the animal hard so that its head struck the stone. After a few more kicks, it lay limp in the boy's hands.

"Wassaja!" a girl's voice called. "You caught another rabbit! A big one! And you are so young!"

The brown boy looked up the slope of the hill. He didn't consider himself young, for he was already six winters old.

"Why, it is nothing," said he. "There are lots of them. They are easy to catch."

The girl, who was slightly larger than Wassaja, ran up close. A smaller girl followed. They too had dark skin and very black hair.

"We've been watching. Over there in the tree."

"I know it. I saw you. It's a wonder you didn't scare everything away with all your moving and chattering."

"Wassaja, we know better than that!" they protested.

Not answering them, the boy began to move downhill, with the girls following in single file. From the way he proudly strutted along, it was plain that he was well pleased with himself.

The children were Iron Mountain Apaches, and they had spoken in the deep-throated language of that tribe. None of the three wore any clothes, even though the October air was chilly. In another week, perhaps two, their mother would give Wassaja and his sisters rough skins or blankets to wear on cloudy days and after sundown, but now it was still warm enough for them to be without clothes. In this part of the country, going naked most of the year was the most comfortable way to live. Even the grown-up men wore only a loincloth, and the women a cloth or a simple dress.

Wassaja had been gone all morning, but he knew that his mother had not been worried, for he was trained to take care of himself. If he could not be on his own, he and all his family would have been ashamed. So now he walked proudly down the slope, around a clump of trees, across the stream, and up the next hill to where the big Apache camp had been built.

With the two girls still behind him, Wassaja marched straight to the wickiup home that his mother had built weeks ago. This was a dome-shaped hut made of poles, dried grasses, reeds, and animal skins. It was only one room, and had a dirt floor. Nearly a hundred similar wickiups were clustered there in the village. Dozens of people could be seen — the children at play, the women working, the men dozing in the late afternoon sun. Smoke from many cookfires had created a bluish cloud that snaked up and around the mountain, but Wassaja paid it no attention. He knew that smoke could be a sign of the presence of enemies. But the Apaches had no enemies.

As Wassaja neared his home, he saw his mother outside, standing beside a large pottery vessel she had made. It hung over a small fire and she was stirring what Wassaja knew would be a tasty stew. He ran to her. Strong, and tall for age six, bronzed skin glistening in the sun glow, black hair bouncing off his shoulders, he moved without effort. His face was rounded "like the full moon," his mother had once told him with a smile. Sometimes he fancied himself a creature of the wilderness, and truly he had the grace of a wild animal.

The mother smiled at her handsome son. She was a young woman, straight and proud of bearing, and very pretty, too. The boy often thought that her name, Thilgeya, was the most beautiful that he had ever heard. "It is like the song of a bird," he once told her, and she had seemed pleased.

"You have brought something for dinner?" she asked, her eyes sparkling as she reached for the rabbit. With quick motions of a knife, she slit its hide down the white belly and then skinned it. Next she stuck the knife point into a blood vessel, removed the knife, and held her finger over the cut.

"Killing is not always good," the mother said soberly, as she worked. "But you must kill for food. And here is your reward — take it and drink."

Wassaja took the skinned rabbit and quickly put his mouth over the opened blood vessel. He sucked. He sucked and swallowed once, twice, three times.

"Please, Wassaja," the biggest girl spoke up. "I am your sister. I should have some."

"Do not bother him, Cowowsapucha," the mother said quietly.

Wassaja swallowed twice more, enjoying the rich warm blood. Then, touched by his sister's pleading eyes, he passed the rabbit on to her. She sucked and swallowed, and smiled her pleasure. Presently her eyes turned toward the smaller sister, who was watching hopefully.

"Me?" the little one pleaded.

"Yes, Wholaccah," the mother nodded. "Cowowsapucha, you must give her some, too."

"It is good to catch food for your sisters. Your father will be proud."

"I could always get rabbits for Cowowsapucha and Wholaccah. It is a man's place to do so," said Wassaja.

The girls smiled and the mother laughed gently. "You are far from a man," the older girl said.

Wassaja drew himself up proudly and glared. "I can shoot the arrow straight!"

"A *small* arrow. A child's bow," the others laughed.

"And kill with the tomahawk."

"A coyote puppy, maybe, or a raccoon," said his sisters.

At last, the mother scolded the girls. "Stop teasing your brother. He will be a man in time."

Encouraged, Wassaja bragged more loudly still. "I will soon go on raids with the other men. And I will bring home a Pima slave. The Apaches are *N'de* (The People)! Don't you understand?" He thrust out his chin, in what he imagined to be a fierce look. By now there was quite an audience, and everyone knew that he was imitating his father and the other elders of the village.

The mother nodded her approval. The Apaches were indeed the most powerful tribe. They looked up to no one. The Pima Indians had been their victims many times. Often, Wassaja's father let him sit at the great council fires and had taught him the tribal history and the war dances. All of it was training, he knew, for fighting other, weaker folk. Sometimes when he walked the streets of his village, watching the big, bronzed, muscular warriors, he wished he might grow up at once.

"I will fight the Pimas," he boasted louder still, now pretending to swing a deadly tomahawk. "Our people have always spit on them and laughed at them. They are weak farmers."

"We take their vegetables and grain for food," Wassaja's mother tried to explain. But she couldn't quiet her son. "We Apaches must rule all," he cried. "The other tribes fear us and hate us and can do nothing to stop us!"

The other children were impressed, especially Wassaja's own little sister. "My brother," she said, "will the Pimas not come some day and seek revenge?"

"Hoo! Let them try it! They could never do us any harm."

CHAPTER 2

Terror
at Dawn

Dinner that sundown was especially good. Wassaja sat with the others under an oak tree, the earthen pot of stew before them. It had cooked down so that it was thick. When it cooled, Cocuyevah the father began to eat.

He dipped in a hand up to his thumb, took out part of the rabbit, and ate it with pleasure. The others watched. He dipped in again, and again and then Wassaja caught his eye. Presently the father nodded to the boy, gesturing toward the pot.

Wassaja eagerly moved closer and dipped in his own hand. For ten minutes or more, father and son relished the rich, hot food. The pot held some venison, a leg of dog, and Wassaja's rabbit. Jojoba nut meal had been added, too.

When the man and the boy had finished, both moved away from the pot, content. Now the mother and her two daughters ate. Not much was left for them, but the mother found some dried cakes she had cooked of acorn meal, and these were crumbled in the remaining stew juice. The women were used to eating what their men left.

After supper, the Apache men and boys all gathered

at a central campfire in the village. Soon one of the younger men began a ritual dance, lasting three or four minutes. Then he sat down. Cocuyevah looked at Wassaja and gestured with his head.

"You, son," said he. "You have learned our dances. And you have been a good hunter this day."

The boy jumped up eagerly, his face serious. This was not a dance of fun — it was more nearly a religious ceremony. Wassaja stood motionless in the firelight for a long moment. Then, slowly, he began chanting. His was a strong voice, but still that of a child. The sound was an easy, well-known rhythm:

EE-yah, yah-yah
EE-yah, yah-yah
EE-yah
EE-yah
EE-yah, yah-yah

The syllables seemed to come from deep inside him. His face was very grave, his eyes almost glazed. With the chanting he began a dance step, moving with grace and ease, a kind of step-hop, step-hop, with a gentle swaying, and very little motion of the arms. The dance did not last long, and soon he sat back down. One or two old men nodded approval.

While others danced, there was talk, much of it again boasting of the Apaches' great record in warfare and their unconquerable strength. As Wassaja sat there beside his father in the warmth of the fire, he felt an immense pride. He was a part of N'de, one of The People. But as the fire gradually died to coals, and stars gemmed the sky more brightly than ever, he began nodding with sleep. He felt Cowowsapucha touch his shoulder. "Come," the sister murmured.

Together they went to their home and found their way inside, despite the darkness there. With no words, he and the two girls moved to their side of the wickiup and crawled into a pile of buffalo and deer skins on the floor. Presently the mother and father came in and wriggled under their own pile of bedding.

Almost at once Wassaja heard the measured breathing of his sisters, telling him that they slept. In barely a moment he heard Cocuyevah gently snoring. He did not know if his mother went to sleep quickly, but he himself did not. Lying there on the bedding, close to the earth, he could gaze out the wickiup door with its top fringe of straw against the starlit sky. This was always a pleasure, for the sky was the most beautiful of all things. It seemed ever alive. The stars and the moon were never still, but spent the night hunting, though he knew not what kind of game they sought. Even when it was storming, the sky was alive. The straw and skins of the wickiup would not stop much rain, but since it did not storm often here, he felt safe and secure. Wassaja smiled a bit to himself, happy in his mind. He had won favor for his trapping skill this day. He had been allowed to do one of the ritual dances before the elders. Life was good.

Finally, Wassaja turned away from the starry sight, and with a sigh, dropped off to sleep.

He could not — ever afterward — know just how long he slept there. Later he supposed that the awakening came about an hour before dawn.

It was a strange noice — a crackling sound — that caused it. It went *snap . . . swiss-s-ss . . . crack . . . snap . . . SWISS-S-S-SSSSS CRACKLE*. Rapidly, it grew louder.

Against the morning chill he had snuggled down under an old tanned animal skin, so that he could see nothing at all. But the strange sound frightened him. Moreover, there was an alarming new smell. He threw the cover back.

"FATHER!" The boy shouted at once. "FIRE!"

At almost the same moment he heard a scream outside.

Several people began shouting, and then things began to happen faster than he could understand them, with many loud sounds.

"GET OUT, GET OUT!" somebody shouted, and a woman began to scream in terror.

He felt a great stirring as the people in his wickiup began to scramble up. Smoke started him coughing, lights were flashing, and all around him fires crackled and burned. Wassaja, first on his feet, saw that one entire side of their wickiup was blazing. He could see dozens of forms running outside, then realized that almost every other home was burning, too.

His eyes were full of the sight before him, but he felt his parents and sisters leap to their feet and stand beside him, all stared for a moment in wide-eyed horror. Then as they began to choke in the smoke and heat, the family darted through the blazing door. The father, Cocuyevah, led the way.

Thwup!

An arrow streaked out of the darkness. With tremendous force, it went through the father's abdomen.

Crazed with fear now, Wassaja ran blindly for a few moments before he remembered to look back for his mother and sisters. But they were not in sight. He turned right and left to search, crying and sobbing.

Hundreds of his people were screaming or shouting and running in all directions. Not finding his family, he too began to run aimlessly.

But only for a moment. The next instant, Wassaja stopped in horror. Before him were four strange demons. Demons — supernatural creatures such as he never imagined — plainly had come out of the roaring fires.

Each demon had a body like that of a huge buck deer, but without horns. And more frightening still, from the back of each grew the body, arms, and head of a man!

The creatures were horses ridden by Indian warriors, but Wassaja could not know this. He had never seen a horse before. He shrieked in horror at the nightmarish things.

The boy began to run again, but tripped and almost fell into a fire. He couldn't see his mother or sisters, but all around him were many other people of all ages who were running or being slaughtered by the demons. Hundreds of arrows whizzed from the surrounding darkness. The great creatures raced after people on foot and struck them down with tomahawks.

Wassaja turned right. He saw nowhere to go, no hint of safety anywhere, but instinct made him flee toward the forest and away from the fires.

Then he heard a clatter of hoofs behind him, and a man's voice arose in a victory shout — "Hee-YAH-H-H-H-HHHHHH, YOW-YOW!"

Others took up the shout and it echoed through the wilderness, even above the screams of the Apaches and the crackling of the fires.

Next instant Wassaja saw one of the great stag-like

demons skid to a halt at his very side. He heard the shout again. The man-body of the demon reached down an arm and grabbed Wassaja by the hair of his head. The boy rose into the air and then fell astride the demon's main body, in front of the human form. Again the demon began to shout and run.

The boy was almost unconscious from sheer terror. But he caught a glimpse of the whole Apache camp blazing to the sky, the few remaining Apaches being hit by arrows or struck down by tomahawks. Surely, this must be the end of the world.

And in a way, for him, it was.

Wassaja saw no more for a long time. The demon galloped off with the boy, yelling "EE-YAH-H-H-H-HHHHHH, YOW-YOW-YOW!" and all the world seemed to drift away from him.

CHAPTER 3

Captive Child

It seemed to Wassaja that his head was hanging over a cliff, and that somebody was rubbing his legs and his stomach. He tried to open his eyes, but the lids seemed much too heavy. Once he murmured "Father," but heard no response.

The rubbing continued, and the boy slowly realized that all his body was moving. And he could now tell that what had seemed a distant rumble was really the sound of many voices. Wassaja tried opening his eyes again. Yes, he could do it now. And — daylight had come! Where on earth was he? He had to blink twice to make his eyes focus. Lifting his hands, he felt a strong arm around his stomach. He saw an animal's huge head bobbing just in front of him, and felt the animal walking. Suddenly it came to Wassaja that he was on the animal's back. He twisted to look around and up — right into the grinning face of a man.

The demon!

It had to be! His mind suddenly cleared and the fear returned. The demon had him. He looked into that face once more. It was not Apache, so he knew it had to be Pima. His father had often described the Pima people, with their flatter faces and their humped posture. This demon figure fit it all perfectly. So, then, the Pimas were half animal, half man. His father had not told him that. Perhaps Father had not wanted to frighten him.

And yet, unbelievably, he was not injured; he had no pain. He seemed to be hanging limply in the Pima demon's arms, still astride its main lower body. He forced himself to sit erect and look around.

Two dozen or so other demons walked near him. Following them walked or trotted a crowd of brown men, all grinning and talking happily. So, maybe only the Pima chieftains were man-animal demons. Both groups were carrying burdens. Some pulled or pushed girls along — girls from his own village! Again his heart leaped.

Now he understood! The Pimas had raided the Apache village on Iron Mountain. They had come to burn and rob and kill. His own father had been struck down by an arrow! Doubtless these girls were to become Pima slaves. He looked carefully but could not see his sisters or his mother. He recalled how the Apache men had felt so scornful of the Pimas, and had felt so strong and safe that no night guard had been kept around the camp. That had spelled disaster.

"Now I am a captive, too," he murmured.

It was a disgraceful and shameful thought. Yet it was true. He, Wassaja, of the proud N'de knew himself to be in the hands of demons. At long last the Pimas had gotten revenge.

He rode with these fearful thoughts for a long while before another great truth came to him. The demon stopped, and to the boy's astonishment, the upper part of the demon detached itself from the lower part!

The upper part slid off and took Wassaja with it. That part then became a man just like the other men walking along. It was unbelievable. Surely no living creature could divide itself into two parts! He stared, mouth open and eyes wide, especially at the demon's lower part. It was brown almost like the men, and its head was like that of a buck deer, only much heavier. Suddenly the head shook itself and snorted, causing Wassaja to jump back in fresh alarm. The men all laughed.

The boy kept staring. He saw that the demon had legs and hoofs, but its hoofs were round, not split or pointed. It was bigger than any deer, though not as high as an elk. It had a long bushy tail, and hair near its head that was tangled with dirt. A rope woven of plant fibers went around its nose in a loop. The creature lowered its head and began to eat grass.

Suddenly Wassaja felt the world begin to whirl around him. Such discoveries were more than his young mind could stand, and a strange numbness came over him. He didn't even know it when his body hit the ground.

When he again came to his senses, he was in a village somewhat similar to his own home camp that had burned. The homes here were different from Apache houses. They were square huts of mud and sticks, flat on top. But the cookfires and the children and the dogs and the dirt were like those of the Apaches. There were no trees here such as those he knew near his own camp. The few that he did see were little more than bushes. They had a few tiny leaves and many thorns. The air was much warmer here than on Iron Mountain.

Presently Wassaja found himself eating stew. It was not unlike that made by his mother, and he was very hungry. A red-brown woman gave it to him in a little earthen bowl. She spoke in a language he did not understand.

The sun had climbed to the top of the sky and was on its way down the other side before Wassaja began to hope that he would not be killed. He decided that maybe — just maybe — he would be kept alive to live here in the Pima village as a slave. He knew that girls were sometimes taken into slavery, but the elders had always told him that any male captives were tortured and then slain.

The boy would have cried about his fate, except that Apaches were taught not to cry. Grimly, he clenched his teeth together, drew a deep breath, and stood tall. He would remain proud no matter what.

But to his surprise, nothing much happened.

That night he was put to bed with Pima children in one of their huts. At dawn, he was fed again. This second day, the Pima children did tease him a little. They threw clods of dirt at him, and laughed. They poked him with sticks, and laughed again. One of the bigger boys openly wet on him, and that seemed funniest of all to the others. The grown-up Pimas laughed at this, too. Wassaja did not fight back. He merely tried to dodge when he could. In the end, he was not really harmed at all, except in spirit. He knew that he was fortunate. In the Apache camp, an enemy captive would surely have been made to suffer pain. Such was the way of life there. These Pimas, he felt, were a softer people — and how fortunate this was for him!

By the end of the week, Wassaja knew that the

Pima chieftains were not two-headed demons; they were simply men. That animal part was a *horse!* The white man's horse, which he had often heard about.

Here he saw Pima men and boys riding every day. He watched them make cages of those fiber ropes to go around each horse's head, with strings to hold for controlling the horse. Big boys would spring to the animals' backs, kick their sides, and streak away faster than he had dreamed was possible. It was truly an exciting thing to watch. He longed to try that ride himself.

Moreover, the Pima food was the best he had ever known. It seemed to come in many kinds. All of his life, Wassaja had lived mostly on meat and a kind of nut meal and the rich sweet "candy" made of cooked-down maguey leaves. One reason the Apache camp was on Iron Mountain was because of the abundance of maguey plants growing there. He had often helped his mother harvest the fat leaves and dig a pit for baking them.

But here he had gruels and breads made of dried mesquite beans, plus other things he did not recognize. One was a white substance called flour. He did not see the Pimas harvest or kill anything from which to make flour. It seemed to grow in a small bag that was inside a bigger bag made of skins. The Pimas also ate a strange green stew made of leaves that were pulled from the ground. It was boiled with the meat of rabbits and birds, and it tasted wonderful.

He lived in the home of the demon — no, the man — who had snatched him up by his hair that night of the massacre. This was a man no older than his father Cocuyevah, and it was clear that he owned Wassaja

Lakewood Elementary School
6745 Hwy 79 N.
Buchanan, TN 38222

now. After his first week here, the boy could understand a little of what the man said to him.

One morning Wassaja's owner put the cage on his
horse's head and then motioned to Wassaja. The boy,
though frightened, half hoped that he might be allowed
to ride alone, as Pima boys did. He came forward
slowly, and then the big man lifted him astride the
horse. Wassaja trembled a bit from excitement. He
smiled, looking around. Would he be allowed to ride
alone?

No. The man swung up behind him and kicked the
horse in the ribs with his heels. The horse obediently
started walking. Wassaja filled his hands with the
long dirty mane and held on, and the man behind
kept him steady. It was no ride on a demon this time;
he was actually riding a white man's horse! Wassaja
truly wished that his friends back in the Iron Mountain
village might see him. But no, he remembered, there
was no village now. It had burned. Probably his
parents and sisters were dead. Wassaja grew immensely
sad and lonely. And he was also confused and afraid.
Still, if ever he managed to find his mother and sisters
and any of his friends, he would have much to tell.

The ride that day lasted until the sun ranged far
toward its bed. Late in the afternoon, Wassaja saw a
very strange village ahead of them. It was not made
of Apache houses nor of Pima homes, but of things
quite new to him. His mind could not take it all in
at once. Many people were to be seen in the village,
but they were far, far different from either the Apaches
or the Pimas.

Then, suddenly, young Wassaja knew that he was
face to face with hundreds of white people!

CHAPTER 4

For Thirty
Silver Dollars

Wassaja could only stare, his mouth open in wonder.

"They have hair on their *faces!*" he told himself. "And their eyes are light brown, or blue like the sky!"

Certainly white people were far different from any people he had ever seen or even imagined. The face hair interested him most. Apache men had only a few facial hairs, but here almost every man's face was covered. Many white men had only their eyes and noses showing through fuzzy growth. The hair on the Indians' heads was long and coarse and black. These whites were like birds — decorated in light brown, dark brown, red, yellow, gray, and even white. His mother's hair hung below her shoulders, graceful and free. Here the women piled their hair on top of their heads, in strange knots.

These whites also wore more than breech cloths or blankets. They wore skins — or something, he couldn't be sure what — that covered them from neck to toe. The boy had never thought before of covering his body. But as he looked around at the people, he saw three or four white boys his own size staring at him and grinning. They too were covered from head to toe with baggy "skins," and each of them wore an odd thing on top of his head. For some reason, they made his nakedness seem strange. He wondered why. The air was not cold, so the body should be free. Wassaja sensed that these white people were not as intelligent as N'de.

"They smell queer, too," the Apache boy told himself, his nose twitching. "Not like N'de. And many of the men have brown spit. They are chewing something brown. Some of them suck on a burning stick and blow out smoke! Why on earth would anyone want to do such a thing?"

Wassaja had ridden long in the sunshine with his Pima owner, so he was very thirsty. But he saw no water, and nobody offered him any. And he forgot about it in the amazement of his discoveries here.

He heard many people speak in a strange language.

"Ho! So you want to sell your little naked 'Pache, hey?" a big white man boomed to the Pima man.

"Me sell," the Pima agreed.

Wassaja understood nothing. He simply stared, almost hypnotized. Soon he found himself the center of a crowd of men and women and boys and girls, all of whom were white.

"Where'd you git him?" another paleface asked.

"Me sell," the Pima repeated.

Everybody seemed to be looking at him. A white woman wearing a strange thing on her head that almost hid her face from him came and put her arm around Wassaja. Then she took off a part of her dress.

"It's shameful, him this way," she said. "Here, little man, I'll just tie my apron around you."

The white men laughed, and Wassaja felt her tie

the cloth high around his chest and drape it like a breechcloth. Suddenly he felt proud. This must mean that they thought him older, big enough to wear clothes. So, it was an honor. He would not have gotten a breechcloth for a long time yet, at home on Iron Mountain.

"Cain't talk, too little to do much work," one man spoke up. "What good would he be if a person did buy him?"

"He's a captive, I vow," said another. "Don't look like a Pima. Stands taller. Harder face. I did hear there was a big massacre a while ago."

People pressed closer to Wassaja, grinning as they watched the sale of the young Indian boy. Wassaja was thirstier, and he was hungry now, but he too rather enjoyed the gathering here. He felt himself to be the important center of attention, and he tried to look proud, holding his head high.

Thus the talk and the looking kept on for a long while. Nobody fed the boy or brought him any water, and his lips began to feel parched. But he had been trained at home never to complain when he was suffering any physical need, so he simply waited.

At times he looked over the people's heads at the fronts of what must be their homes. The wickiups seemed to be made of some kind of flat limbs from trees. A few of them were not wood colored, but were white or red like rocks. Other houses were made of brown dirt stacked into walls. Wassaja saw their dogs and their horses, and he wondered where their cookfires were. Some things seemed familiar, but he couldn't understand much of the white man's world.

Then, something extremely odd caught his attention. These white people actually had wickiups that rolled and rattled along on big round feet! They were pulled along by horses, and some of the horses were more like short, fat antelope because they had horns and moved very slowly. He gasped as he saw other rolling wickiups that were pulled by horses with huge ears like those of jackrabbits. What a mysterious world! He knew that his relatives would never believe what he would tell them if ever he got home again.

Thinking about home, Wassaja again felt very lonely. He was also extremely thirsty and hungry. As he stood there, his face set hard, a white man riding on one of those rolling wickiups came close to the crowd. His wickiup was somewhat like a short fat caterpillar. It was wrinkled a bit, and was gray-white on top. In its front end — perhaps its mouth — the white man sat holding strings that guided two horses pulling the wickiup. This man was dressed in a dark covering and had a hard black thing on his head.

"Whoa," the man said, pulling on the strings, and the horses stopped.

Wassaja was now able to see the rolling wickiup more clearly. The caterpillar skin was not really skin, but was a kind of woven cloth. On it were some mysterious marks. These appeared to be painted symbols, such as his father often put on himself for the ritual dances before war. The marks looked like this:

Carlos Gentilé

PHOTOGRAPHER

Maybe these were war-dance signs, and maybe this white man was some kind of chieftain who rode the big wickiup with round legs to kill his enemies. Wassaja stared long and hard.

"Ho, Gentilé!" one of the white men near Wassaja called out. "Whoa up, man, and come here! We got something'll interest you."

The man in black looked down from his wickiup seat at the crowd and at the Indian lad.

"This Pima wants to sell a little 'Pache boy, Gentilé. Ain't that something? You wanta take his pitcher?"

"Yeah," another man put in, "why don't you make a photygraft of him?"

The first speaker grinned and said, "Gentilé, you've got no fambly or nothin'. Whyn't *you* buy this little 'Pache, hey?"

The other men all laughed loudly.

"Shore, Gentilé. He'd make you a good fambly. He could be yore servant. WHAW!" The man laughed at what he considered a great joke.

Wassaja looked from face to face, trying to get some hint of what the men were saying. They seemed to be talking about him with the new man. But he couldn't guess what they said.

The new man, Mr. Gentilé, climbed slowly down from his covered wagon. He had not answered, or even smiled. He came toward Wassaja, and the boy saw a kindly look on his face. Still with no words, the man squatted beside the boy to be at eye level with him, then reached out and put a hand on the boy's shoulder. To Wassaja it felt gentle, almost like his mother's touch. He looked the man in the eyes and felt his own lips tremble a bit.

"You say this Pima wants to *sell* him?" Mr. Gentilé asked.

"Shore thing! Taken him captive, wants to sell.

Prob'ly knock him in the head if he don't sell. Looks like slavery's back!"

"Slavery! May God forgive us!" Mr. Gentilé spoke softly, and tenderly. Wassaja felt still more comfortable with him. Plainly this white man's eyes and manner were kind.

"I will buy him," said Mr. Gentilé, standing erect.

"Hanh?" The others were surprised. "You mean it? You'd shore 'nough buy? We was joshin' you, Gentilé."

"How much'll you pay?" another asked.

The Pima man waited nearby, his face a mask of stone. Wassaja looked up at Mr. Gentilé.

"Buy him, raise him up, fatten him, and eat him!" a half-grown white boy teased.

Mr. Gentilé looked hard at the white boy, and the youngster stopped laughing.

"This Indian lad is a human being," said Mr. Gentilé, so softly that the others stopped talking to hear. "There has been a massacre of the Apaches. Likely this child has no people left alive. But he was, and he still is, a child of God, just as you and I."

Wassaja saw him reach inside his coat and pull out a leather bag. The boy wondered what on earth was going on. He frowned a bit as he waited, but he somehow liked this white man in the dark clothes.

"I will pay what I have," said Mr. Gentilé. "Here, Pima, hold out your hands."

The Pima had dealt with white men before. So he reached out with his cupped hands, grinning, to catch the money.

Mr. Gentilé took a handful of silver dollars out of his leather bag. Wassaja saw them as strange, shiny round rocks that made a clinking sound. They must be river rocks, he thought, made shiny by much washing in the sands. They were beautiful.

The boy's eyes were fastened on them as the white man began dropping them one by one into the Pima's hands. He heard another man in the crowd begin counting, "One . . . two . . . three . . . four . . . five." The white men chuckled as the clink and the counting went on. Presently it came to an end, ". . . twenty-seven . . . twenty-eight . . . twenty-nine . . . thirty."

There Mr. Gentilé stopped. He turned his leather bag upside down, showing the Pima that it was now empty. Then he looked into the Pima's face.

"Heck, Gentilé," a white man put in. "If you're serious, you don't have to *buy* this boy. 'Taint legal to do so. Just take him, and we'll run this derned Pima to kingdom come."

"I am not buying a slave," Mr. Gentilé explained. "I am simply paying this Pima for — shall we say — making a delivery. You men were right. I do need a family, for I have been lonely these past years, and I have prayed for one. Perhaps this is God's way of answering my prayers."

Nobody was laughing now. One man quietly exclaimed, "Well, I'll be dad-burned!"

Wassaja looked at the many faces. Their laughter had ceased. One man even removed his hat, and some of the women seemed as if they were about to cry. The boy looked up into Mr. Gentilé's face, and it shone with a gentle smile.

Something inside Wassaja told him that whatever was happening here was somehow good. He felt the gentle grip of the man's fingers on his shoulder. Now the man's arm went around his back and patted him. It caused a new and wonderful feeling.

"Thank you for stopping me," Mr. Gentilé said to the crowd, which was slowly moving back. Then the man turned his face and smiled down at Wassaja.

"Come," said he, softly, "let us go home, my son."

CHAPTER 5

White Man's Magic

Walking off with the white man called Gentilé, Wassaja barely saw the Pima remount his horse and ride away. The boy thought hard about what had happened.

"I have been swapped for those shiny rocks," he decided, thinking fast. "They made a *clink-clink* sound in the Pima's hand. He will use them in his war dances, and will string them into ornaments to wear on his body, as my father would." But he saw no such ornaments on the white man as he turned to look up at him.

So far not one of the white people had hurt the boy. This was a surprise for the Apaches all knew that white people killed Indians whenever they could. Perhaps this white man had been assigned the job of torturing Wassaja. But why, then, had the man been so gentle? Why was his touch, even now as they walked, almost like that of the boy's mother?

Wassaja turned to look back. The other whites stared. One woman took a step or two forward, but then seemed to think better of it and stopped. Wassaja thought she looked a little like his mother, Thilgeya, whose very name haunted him because of its bird-call beauty. Sometimes, since he'd been captured, he would dream of a beautiful bird singing "teel-GAY-yah, teel-GAY-yah" as it flew past him, and he would awake sobbing.

Mr. Gentilé led Wassaja, who was still wearing the apron that the woman had tied on him, to the wickiup with round legs. He lifted the small boy up and put him onto a seat, then climbed up beside him. He picked up several ropes and made a sound, "Tch-tch, giddap! You — Kit, Blue!"

The horses out in front of the wickiup began to walk forward, and the whole thing moved, carrying Wassaja and Mr. Gentilé along. It was a marvelous experience! He wasn't being killed or tortured. He was actually being moved along, sitting up high above the crowd. Wassaja felt his heart thumping with excitement and he began to smile a little for sheer joy.

"Don't be afraid," said Mr. Gentilé. "We'll be home in a minute. Do you understand any English?"

Wassaja gave no answer. He simply looked up at the man.

"No, I expect not, son. But I'll teach you. You are my son now."

The thirst that had grown in him left Wassaja's mouth dry and hurting, yet he could not say so. Hunger rode with him too, for he had not eaten since early dawn, and now it was night. Well, he could only wait.

The moving wickiup soon stopped before another, and larger wickiup that had no legs. It was made of those flat trees he had noticed. There were markings on the front of it just like those on the moving wickiup. Mr. Gentilé helped the boy down, then quickly went to work on the animals in the front of the moving wickiup.

"Whoa boys," the man said, gently.

He untied some leather thongs and unsnapped fastenings. Presently, the horses moved away.

Mr. Gentilé put the horses in a pen and fed them hay, then came and again took Wassaja's hand. He smiled down at the boy.

"We'll have supper," he said. "I'll bet you are hungry. All boys are, I know. Food? You understand food? . . Eat?"

Wassaja said nothing, and Mr. Gentilé sighed.

They stopped at the door of the wickiup and in the twilight the man squatted down to put an arm around the boy again. Then he pointed to himself, touched his chest, and said, "Father . . . father . . . father. Say 'father.' My name is Mr. Gentilé."

Wassaja only stared, puzzled. Plainly the man wanted something of him. He was pointing at himself, then back at the boy's own mouth. Perhaps he wanted him to speak. Well, those other white men had called this one a name, so he tried it.

"zh-tilly," he murmured.

Mr. Gentilé beamed, smiling with joy. "Hey!" he cried. "You said my name! Say it again, son, 'Gentilé'!"

Wassaja pronounced it better this time, "gen-tilly."

"Praise God!" the man exclaimed.

" 'aise god." Wassaja echoed in a low tone.

The man looked startled and happy. "Sa-a-aaay, you're going to learn fast! You catch every sound I make. My son! My own son! But first we must eat."

Wassaja understood none of that, but somehow sensed that it was friendly and good.

Mr. Gentilé led him into the wickiup. The boy couldn't see clearly at first, for it was very dark in here. Then, *scrat-t-tch!*

Strange new magic had been made! The man, Gentilé, had scraped his forefinger along a wall, and suddenly there was a flame of fire at the end of the finger! Impossible! Unbelievable! But true!

Now the man took a round piece of ice off another piece of ice, and touched the flame to the bottom part. It burned there! He put the first piece of ice over the flame, and the whole room glowed in brilliant light! Wassaja, numbed by this sudden experience, feared he might go unconscious again. He closed his eyes. When he reopened them a moment later, the man was gone.

But he heard Mr. Gentilé nearby. Wassaja realized that he himself was sitting. Mr. Gentilé had put him on a rock — or something — covered with some kind of smooth skins. It was softer than anything he had ever touched. His legs couldn't reach the ground, but he was comfortable. And that magic flame was still gently burning, lighting the whole room.

Wassaja feared the ice would melt and kill the flame, but as he watched, nothing of the kind happened. So, gradually he began to look around. And once more amazement struck him. There, on the inside walls of this paleface man's wickiup-home, were *some dozens of little people staring at him!*

He drew back in fear. But no harm came. The little people, who were about as large as his hand, did not move. They said nothing, but simply gazed hard at him, most of them unsmiling. He saw that the people were white men and women and children dressed in the peculiar way he had seen them dressed outside. But they had no human color. All were in tones of gray and white or brown-gray and white.

So, then, here was a new race of human beings! Wassaja's mind was working hard now.

"They are no bigger than birds," said he, whispering in Apache language. "So they couldn't hurt me."

That gave him courage. Presently he slid out of the soft chair and edged closer to them. They made no move and said nothing. Yet they couldn't be dead little people, for they had their eyes open and they looked very much alive. True, they were oddly *flat,* and that was strange. He moved along the wall to get closer, staring at them all the while in wide-eyed wonder.

Then, wholly without expecting it, he came face to face with another Apache Indian boy his own age and size!

This sent a new wave of excitement shooting through him. Another boy from home! He was somehow familiar, too. Wassaja looked at the boy without moving, and the other boy looked back as motionless as he. Then suddenly Wassaja smiled, and the other boy smiled at the same moment. That was good! That was *very* good, Wassaja knew. If somebody smiled at you, he meant to be friends.

"Hello," Wassaja began, in his Apache tongue. "Were you captured too?"

The other boy *appeared* to speak in the same instant, yet Wassaja heard no words but his own. He paused, staring. The other boy stared back.

"What's your name?"

As he asked that, Wassaja turned his head a little.

In the same instant the other boy turned his head and appeared to speak — yet no sound came.

Astounded, Wassaja stared hard. That other boy, he decided, was not only his own size, but he also looked exactly like Wassaja himself! He had sometimes seen his image reflected in pools of water. Why, he was looking at his own image reflected off the wall of a house!

The discovery sent a chill up his spine. Plainly this was something supernatural. A demon must surely live in this white man's wickiup. Probably it waited here to torture him.

Wassaja screamed in terror, ran to the door, and darted up the street of the town. It was dark but he kept running.

Presently he heard Mr. Gentilé — or was it the demon? — running up behind him.

CHAPTER 6

First
Bath

When he heard the steps behind him, Wassaja ran harder. Then he saw a group of men and women approaching directly ahead. He was trapped. He had no way to turn.

"Wait, wait my son!" Mr. Gentilé called from the rear.

Wassaja squatted beside a picket fence, trying to hide. In a moment, grown-ups were all around. Mr. Gentilé gently lifted him. He was trembling, and was sure the man was going to hurt him.

"He run away, hunh?" another man asked. "I expect he's scared."

"We brought some presents, Mr. Gentilé," a woman said. "Clothes and toys and such like. For your new son."

Wassaja felt himself being carried back to the strange wickiup with the little people and the image of himself on the walls. Well, he'd just have to accept it. If they tortured him or killed him, he couldn't stop them. He was captive for sure.

"We got old Apache Mary here with us," somebody called from the rear of the crowd.

Mr. Gentilé stopped. "Who?"

"Apache Mary. She's an old Apache woman been living near here for years, crippled and all. Some soldiers found her half dead. Figured she might be able to make him talk. You know, in his own tongue."

They went inside the house and stood in a circle around Wassaja. The old woman was urged to go up close. She saw the Apache boy and her eyes shone.

"I greet you, little one," she spoke to Wassaja in his own language.

His heart leaped. Here was somebody he could understand. For the first time in many long days he heard words he knew. He was too surprised to answer at first, and only gazed at her, wondering. He stopped trembling.

Mr. Gentilé, smiling, came to him with a plate of food. The food smelled good but he couldn't eat it. Twice he put pieces of meat into his mouth. He chewed, but no saliva came, and he couldn't swallow. He let the food fall back out.

"What is the matter, little one?" Apache Mary asked, again in his own tongue. "Why won't you eat? These whites offer you food. They mean you no harm."

He answered, slowly, in a low tone. Apache Mary had to lean close to him to hear. Then she stood up and spoke in English to Mr. Gentilé.

"You have given him no water. He is sick from thirst."

"Water?" Mr. Gentilé looked horrified. "Oh! I never thought. Water! How cruel of me!"

Wassaja saw a woman rush out, then return at once bearing a dried gourd with a hole cut in it. She held it to him and he saw that it contained clear water. He needed no second invitation, but took the gourd and drank every drop. When he had finished, he stood there panting for breath. The others all watched, smiling.

Then, suddenly, the water all came back. *Ulp!* *Splash!* It poured out of him onto the floor.

"Oh, shame on us!" a woman cried. "Of course it would make him sick, so much at once when he was so dry. Here, get me some more, and a spoon."

While others cleaned the floor, she spoon-fed him water. Wassaja's huge dark eyes looked gratefully around as the woman spoke tenderly, and as Mr. Gentilé knelt there with an arm around the boy. These people, he decided, acted much like his own parents. They weren't torturing him; they were being kind.

Very soon the food looked good again, and Wassaja started eating, at first slowly, then faster and faster. Truly he was starved.

"He must be exhausted," Mr. Gentilé said. "He is dirty, but it is time he had rest. I will put him to bed and bathe him tomorrow."

Apache Mary translated that for him, and Wassaja looked at the white people gratefully. Then Mr. Gentilé picked him up again and carried him through a door. This too was a discovery. This wickiup was not just one large room, but seemed to be made of several rooms. He did not see the image of himself again, although the little people remained on the walls. None of the big people here paid any attention to them, so the boy decided they must be harmless.

Another flame burned on a white stick inside the second room. But so many people crowded in, gazing at him and smiling, that he couldn't see much else. He felt himself lowered onto what must be a big pile of very soft skins. He sank down into them, and Mr. Gentilé drew a cover over him up to his chin. Then Mr. Gentilé held up his right hand.

Suddenly there was complete silence in the room. The people stopped smiling and bowed their heads. Wassaja stared up àt them, but Mr. Gentilé had his eyes closed while he spoke in a low tone. Presently the speaking ended, and the others all tiptoed out. Mr. Gentilé gently touched him before he too went through the door.

"I'll stay awake, then slip off when they have gone," Wassaja decided. "First I must be very quiet."

He did remain quiet. But the moment to run away never arrived. When he came to his senses again, the room was bright with daylight and Mr. Gentilé was sitting near him, smiling.

"Ho!" the white man said, heartily. "Waking up, my son? You have slept long. Arise and let us have breakfast, eh? Then we shall bathe you and dress you in your new clothes."

He helped Wassaja out of bed and led him into another room. A table there had hot food on it. Birds' eggs! He recognized them, although they must have come from a large eagle. There was white cake stuff, much like the Pimas had eaten. And a black liquid; and for the boy, white liquid like that from a mother dog with puppies. And a bowl with a thick porridge in it.

"Corn meal mush, fellow." Mr. Gentilé was beaming happily, pointing to the bowl. "And this is a spoon. Say it, 'spoon.' You'll eat with that. But first, bow your head, my son. Like this."

Wassaja felt the man reach across and push his

head gently down. Then Mr. Gentilé lowered his own head and spoke some more soft words. It must be another strange white man's ritual. It didn't last long, and at once Mr. Gentilé began eating. Wassaja, who was hungry, imitated the man, using the strange thing called a spoon. It was fun, and the food tasted good.

After breakfast, Wassaja was led out the front door and down the street. The sun was at mid-morning by now, and presently they came to a part of the big village where many people had gathered. A big round thing was filled with water as Wassaja looked on. Remembering his thirst of yesterday, he wondered if they expected him to drink that much. No, they couldn't mean that. He looked up at Mr. Gentilé, who had rolled up his sleeves and was holding a brown rock in his hand.

"Now, son," said he, happily.

Before he quite knew what was happening, Wassaja had been lifted and was standing in that tub of water. Mr. Gentilé dipped his brown rock in the water and rubbed it with a wet rag. As he rubbed, white foam appeared.

"It's not a rock at all," Wassaja told himself. "It's an amole root. It has to be, to make lather that way. He is going to bathe me, as the old Apache woman promised. Of course! This is a religious ceremony, and he will put that white foam on me to make *me* white! From now on I will no longer be an Apache. I will be white of skin like the white man!"

Wassaja then made an important decision. If his own people were dead as he thought, and if he *had* to accept a new life, what greater adventure could there be than to become one of these white men!

CHAPTER 7

Carlos
Montezuma

The bath turned out to be more of a ceremony than Wassaja had expected. As he stood in the tub there, he felt Mr. Gentilé grasp a handful of his long black hair.

Squic-c-ck!

Something made a funny sound.

Squick, squic-c-ck!

He heard it again, and looked around. Mr. Gentilé was holding long strands of Wassaja's black hair that had been cut from his head. He also was holding a forked knife, shining in the sunlight.

"You better delouse him as well as cut his hair off short," a man spoke up. "I got some delousing juice. I'll go git it."

Wassaja was shocked that the whites were cutting the hair that had come down to his shoulders. But as the whacking went on, he could do nothing but stand there and look around. In the crowd surrounding him, he saw no white man or boy with long head hair. Theirs ended in bunches over their ears. Well then, if he was being shorn like that, it must be part of becoming white. He waited patiently while the cutting went on.

The other white man returned with a shiny thing, and Mr. Gentilé poured white water out of it onto Wassaja's head. The boy decided it was another kind of foam, perhaps juice of the amole root. But it smelled different. In fact, it smelled horrible. Mr. Gentilé rubbed it all through Wassaja's shortened hair and even on his body.

"Have to scrub you again to get *this* off," the man said, and began soaping him again.

When it was all done and he had been dried with a big cloth, Wassaja looked down at his legs and his arms. He had been washed twice, and he wasn't white at all! He was still a brown-skinned Apache boy.

"Now put your foot in here, son."

Mr. Gentilé held a strange white cloth with holes in it. This was put around his legs and up around his lower body. Then something went over his arms and shoulders, and yet another and heavier piece of cloth was put around his legs. Wassaja did not know names for these clothes, but he saw that they were much like those worn by white boys.

The clothes themselves were very odd. They seemed to bind him between the legs and under the arms. He *felt* them touching him, everywhere. When he had worn a cloth or a blanket in winter, it had still been loose and free, with room for his body to get plenty of air. How could his body live penned up in this way?

There was a lot more talk around Wassaja. Many people came and gave Mr. Gentilé presents, and all were laughing and plainly enjoying themselves. Wassaja tried to look pleased, but mostly he was confused. He greatly wished the old Apache woman was there to speak his language with him.

"What you aim to do with him, Gentilé?" a big white man asked. "Gonna learn him to take pitchers like you do?"

"In time, perhaps," Mr. Gentilé nodded. "But I want him to be well educated. He must learn to speak English, and to read. My first move will be to honor him with an official name."

The talking and laughing continued while Mr. Gentilé once more guided his son into the wagon seat. He picked up the reins and clucked to Kit and Blue. Wassaja watched every move with interest. He looked up into the man's face, then tried the clucking sound.

"Tch-tch," he said, imitating Mr. Gentilé.

"That's right, fellow! I'll make a drover of you, hey?"

They rode in the wickiup-wagon for a short distance, then stopped at the biggest wickiup of all. This one was twice as high as any others Wassaja had seen. It was all white and had a lot of holes in it, with sheets of ice over the holes. It also had a big fat tree or something on the front of it, growing up right out of the roof. They left the wagon and Mr. Gentilé led him into the door of this great house.

Here again, there were strange actions and talk. Wassaja was confused, but he tried to be quiet. Mr. Gentilé met another man dressed in black cloth, and they looked long at the boy.

"You have done a Christian deed by taking in this boy," the other man said. "God will bless you."

"I am not unselfish. I wanted a family, a son."

The other man nodded. "Of course. But you took in a child who might have been lost otherwise. And now you want me to help you name him."

The other man was cupping his chin in his hand as he gazed down at the boy. Wassaja looked up at him and both smiled.

"He is a very strong young man. Perhaps he would have been a chieftain. Indeed, he may yet become one in our white world. So, as to a name, we must not saddle him with anything common. He has had an unusual start in life. I think I have an idea. Are you familiar with Montezuma, the famous leader of the Aztecs in Mexico? He was in power when Cortez invaded Mexico in 1519."

Mr. Gentilé nodded.

"Your own first name is Carlos. If he is to be your son, I suggest Carlos Montezuma as a name for him."

"I'd like that," Mr. Gentilé said, nodding. "It would be his own name, yet it would also be a part of mine."

Wassaja looked from one to the other with increasing interest. He watched as the man in black reached onto a shelf and took down a strange black object, putting it on a wooden table in front of him. The man opened the black object. It seemed to be some kind of box, yet it had a lot of thin white skins inside of it, stacked on one another.

The man took a little stick and dipped one end into some black water held in a little shiny black rock. The stick then became a thing with which to make marks. Wassaja leaned over closer, his eyes wide.

"This is to certify," Mr. Gentilé began saying while he looked at the black marks, "that Carlos Montezuma, Son of Apache Tribe, was baptized at Florence, Arizona, on the seventeenth day of November in the year 1871. Signed: The Reverend A. Echallier."

Mr. Gentilé squatted to be at eye level with Wassaja, then he spoke again.

"Son, you are now Carlos Montezuma, you understand? Say it — 'Carlos Montezuma'." He touched the boy's chest with a finger.

The boy looked long into the man's eyes. Plainly the man wanted something. Did he want him to imitate those sounds? Mr. Gentilé was poking a finger into him as he made the strange noises. Was this to be Wassaja's name? The boy tried to copy the man's words.

"Carloth M'n-zuma," he murmured.

"That's it, that's it!" cried Mr. Gentilé, hugging the boy to him in a bearlike embrace. "Carlos Montezuma — my adopted son! From now on I'll teach you *every*thing!"

The second man spoke. "Will you stay in Arizona, Mr. Gentilé?"

"No sir, I think it best that we go East. I feel that the people here may influence the boy in a bad way. Travel itself can be an education and my wagon is equipped for camping. I can teach him what I know. And no more shall I be lonely."

The second man smiled approval. *"Vaya con Dios,"* he said.

Carlos Montezuma wondered if that was the man's name. Then Mr. Gentilé took the boy's hand and led him back to their wagon.

"We must go, son," his new father said. "We must make ready for traveling."

CHAPTER 8

Eastward
Ho!

It was dawn, with the big red eye of day slowly opening ahead of them. Carlos sat on a folded quilt so that the wagon seat felt soft under him. His white father held the reins, and the horses' heads bobbed rhythmically in the crisp morning air.

"I will count the new day," he told Mr. Gentilé.

He kicked off his leather shoes (strange, strange things to put on one's feet!) and his black stockings. Next he held up two fists, and starting with the left thumb, lifted one finger at a time.

"Owl, buzzard, eagle, crow, jay . . . hawk, sparrow, mockingbird, quail, dove." He spoke the English words very seriously.

Then he leaned to touch his toes one at a time. "Squirrel, chipmunk, fox, rabbit, deer . . . antelope, panther, coyote, bobcat — that's today."

Pausing, he looked up at Mr. Gentilé. Carlos very much wanted the man's approval. Actually, he had started this way of counting — by naming his fingers and toes — two years ago. His Indian mother and father had been pleased. And over the past few days, the new white father had helped him give the toes and fingers English names.

"Correct," said Father now. "And how many days is bobcat?"

Carlos squinted, trying to think. Finally he replied, "Ni—nine ten?"

"Good, good. Only it's nine*teen*."

"Nineteen."

"That's it. You have done well, my son. It is only nineteen days since I found you, and already we can talk to one another with ease. Now let's go on with your nature lesson, as we ride along. I'll point, and you name."

"Yes sir. I like that." Carlos smiled. This was always fun.

The man pointed with his whip. "What is that?"

"Horse. I know horses now!"

"Right, son. And that one?"

"Three."

"No, three is a number — this many." The man held up three fingers. "One, two, *three*. That's a —"

"Tree!" Carlos beat him to it.

"Correct! Tree. But what kind of tree?"

"Pine."

"And that one?"

"Juice. No, spoo — spoose . . . spoon . . . spuice?" The boy was trying hard.

"You're getting it, fellow. Watch my lips. Sp-ruce. Like 'juice' only with a *sp* sound in front, instead of a *juh* sound. Now try it."

"Spu-iss . . . spoose . . . *spruce!*"

"That's it, that's it! You're doing fine. Now what's that?" The man pointed again.

"Grass. For the horses."

"That?"

"Bird." The boy's answer came quickly.

"There?"

"Water."

The lesson continued to be fun. It seemed to Carlos that his father enjoyed it as much as he. When Father ran out of questions, Carlos asked them and Father answered. Presently the man asked again.

"Who made us, Carlos?" he said.

"God."

"Where is God?"

"Here, in the sky, everywhere."

"That is correct. Now *what* is God?"

"Love, you said."

"Yes. God is Love. God made us and He loves us. Do you truly understand that?"

"Yes sir." Carlos hoped he did; but he wasn't sure. He wanted so much to please.

"Do you really understand about love? Do you understand that I love you, my son? Do you remember what I have tried to teach you about it?"

"Yes sir. It's what a father feels for his son. Or what a son feels for his father. And his mother, too?"

"Hmmmmm, yes. Yes, Carlos. For his mother, if he has one."

"My mother is dead?"

"I expect so. That life is over. You are in the white world now."

Carlos wasn't sure he understood all that the man told him, but he said nothing. Besides, he had learned that Father often seemed not to want an answer to his words.

He leaned back in the wagon seat, touching the gray-white canvas that flapped loosely there in the front end. He loved this covered wagon. It was a magic thing. They slept in it, rode in it, ate in it on occasions, and kept many things in it. One part held food for the horses. A big keg of water rode just outside. The front even had a closed-in place that Father called his darkroom, and he'd go in there and come out with pictures. Oh it was a magic thing for sure! But then, Father had said it was only a beginning. He would soon see even more wonderful things.

"We're going east," Father had said, "into the rising sun."

The days passed rapidly, and they were completely happy ones. Never in all his dreams had Carlos imagined a friendship as grand as this with his new father. They rolled and bounced through the forests, over the red and golden hills, across the fields, and into great emerald forests again. Dawn saw them already through breakfast and moving. Each hour the boy learned something new and wonderful.

When he had a mind to, he slept. He'd drop off, leaning against his father, or his head in the man's lap. Sometimes he'd sleep back in the wagon bed under the canvas, on their quilts. Then he'd awaken, slide over the rear of the wagon, and trot alongside the wagon wheels.

Heeist! He'd whistle to the horses through his teeth, as Mr. Gentilé did. Kit and Blue paid no attention to this, but it was fun anyway. He never tired of watching the big animals, and he'd hum little tunes that matched the rhythm of their feet.

Carlos would run along throwing rocks at things. He'd race on ahead and drink from a cool stream before the wagon got there, then wade into it, sloshing the water and kicking it head high and laughing out of sheer joy. Sometimes, afterward, when he was riding in the wagon seat again, he'd quiet down and wonder at himself. So soon, it seemed, he'd forgotten his old life as an Indian. Often, he would just sit staring up at this man he had learned to call Father.

Then one morning something happened that he was to remember all his life. The shock of it came without warning. He was skipping and jumping along not ten steps from the wagon, when *BANG!*

Why, a bolt of lightning must have struck the front of the wagon! A great clap of thunder had sounded there, too.

Carlos dropped to earth, then rolled and disappeared in a clump of brush. His heart was pounding. He lay utterly motionless for a long moment.

"Got him," Mr. Gentilé called. "We'll have plenty of fresh meat now. Come on son, let's skin him."

The boy didn't move, and it took a few minutes for the man to find him. Carlos looked up through the leaves and saw Father holding a long black stick. The horses had stopped, willing to rest.

"Son? . . . Carlos?"

The man stopped over him, then suddenly straightened back up. A look of horror came over his face.

"Oh, may heaven forgive me! I have not told you about guns! I expect you never heard one shoot before."

It was true. Carlos had never, never imagined such a fantastic thing as a hollow stick that gave forth fire and shot out a hard little rock so fast that it could go through animals and kill them.

Father worked hard trying to explain, and Carlos

asked no questions. It was as if he were numbed by it all. He gazed up at Father with wide brown eyes as the two went to the fallen deer. Another piece of white man's magic had been shown. This was a miracle, for sure.

Mr. Gentilé became quiet and thoughtful. He ceased talking as he cleaned the carcass and put it in the wagon. When it was all done, Carlos climbed up into the wagon seat and waited. Father did not join him at once, but went instead into the forest and stood there alone beside the great trees. Presently Carlos heard him talking in a low tone, as if to himself.

After a short while Father came back, climbed up beside him, and took the reins. The boy, curious, looked up at him.

"Son," said the man, very gently, "the world of white people is far from perfect. I know you will not understand all that I say now, but you will understand later. Please do not judge us too harshly."

He paused, but got no answer. Carlos was waiting, listening.

"This gun I have told you about would be a blessing if we used it only for obtaining food."

Carlos had caught a new word. "Its name is Blessing, sir?"

"No, it is called a rifle. This is a rifle. There are other kinds of guns. You will learn of them in time."

Carlos saw that the man seemed strangely sad. He had never known him to look so — so different. It was as if he gazed far off, and saw something that worried him. "Any of these guns might kill a deer. Or — may heaven help us — a man."

"They can kill a man? Would they kill a Pima?"

Father straightened up. His chin went firm. He clapped the reins down on Kit and Blue.

"My son, we shall say no more of it. Not for now. I have seen man fight against man without cause in the East and here in the magnificent West. But you are young. I will not have your brain soiled!"

Carlos did not understand, but Father said no more to him about the long black gun named Rifle. As Mr. Gentilé put the gun back into the wagon, Carlos looked back at Rifle. He thought long about it. It must be a thunder gun because truly it had made thunder and lightning. As lightning often does, it had killed.

The boy sighed long and noisily. Well, he was not surprised. This father of his — all the white people, in fact — could do just about everything he could imagine. There were the pictures and photographs. And the sheet ice named Glass that would never melt, even when it got hot. Carlos could take the thunder Rifle in stride.

CHAPTER 9

Since Time
Began

They ate a cold lunch — ham, bread, and a
raw onion apiece — and then traveled on. They hadn't
talked much for quite a while, for Father seemed lost
in his thoughts. In the silence, Carlos began studying
things that moved past the wagon. This was a never-
ending pleasure. Whenever he rode up in the springy
seat of the covered wagon, the whole world seemed to
march by for him to enjoy. Everything seemed friendly.
Even the trees reached out their arms, wanting to
shake hands. Carlos had been taught to shake hands
with friends, and now he reached out and shook
hands with a young spoose . . . spuiss . . . *spruce!* It
could be a boy tree like me, Carlos thought.

"That's a Christmas Tree, I bet," said Father.

"Sir?"

"Christmas Tree. The kind we decorate. Oh, I
declare, I have not told you about Christmas!"

"No sir. Is she my white mother, maybe?"

Father looked down at him, startled. His mustache
was wriggling, a sure sign that the man was amused.
Carlos saw his lips tighten under the black hairs,
which were moving in and out. For a long moment
the only sound was the *cree-eak-clack, cree-eak-clack*

of the wagon and a mouselike squeak of the seat springs.

"No," Father said, at long last. "Christmas is not your mother. Though in a way, it is the mother of us all."

Much talk followed. Carlos felt that he had never before been so interested in what Father said. It lasted for hours, with many interruptions. But at bedtime that night, the boy told himself that he knew all there was to know about another white boy, one named Jesus.

"Je-suss." He tried out the name, saying it softly to himself, again and again. There under the quilts, he felt Father reach over and pat him fondly on the shoulder. He felt very comfortable, but he wasn't sleepy. He kept thinking.

Father had said something about a Star in the East. Well, they were traveling toward the East. Maybe he'd get to meet this Jesus! And maybe they could play together. Carlos felt that he would surely like Jesus. He decided to save up some of the prettiest of the colored stones he had collected, as a gift for the white boy. He fell asleep, planning it.

Next dawn brought new interests. The two had camped near a cold stream, so both Carlos and Father shucked off their nightgowns and plunged in with a great *whooshing* and shouting and laughing. The cold water lifted their spirits and it also made Carlos extremely hungry.

"I declare, my son, you eat more than I do!" Father smiled, offering him another piece of meat. It was greasy bacon, cooked over coals on a green stick. Carlos pulled it off with a fork, onto his tin plate.

Bread, too, was cooked on green sticks. Father would mix the dough, give him a roll of it, and he would twist it around the stick. Then Carlos would hold it near the fire — not close enough to burn, just near enough to rise quickly, cook through, and turn brown. The bread and the bacon together were delicious.

More dawns passed; more leisurely days rolled by. Carlos felt that the world was wonderful, and that he couldn't have been happier. Before he quite realized it, the sun had changed its path through the heavens. Carlos had meant to count the full moons, but every day and night had been much too exciting to remember about counting. Father said they had ridden hundreds of miles.

Then came a day of sadness. They had been traveling in an open country without many trees when they came to another white man's town. This was a Spanish town, Father said, and it was named Santa Fe. While Carlos was admiring the people's strange costumes and trying to understand their strange language, Father sold his team and wagon.

Carlos was horrified. "Do you mean we have to leave Kit and Blue?" he cried out.

Father tried to comfort him. "We will ride in something even grander than a wagon, son. It is called a stagecoach. And then — you'll like this! — then, an *iron horse* for us!"

Carlos showed interest. "Iron horse?" he asked, his eyes wide.

"Yes sir. I promise." Father explained only enough to make it sound very mysterious. "Wait and see. You'll have the surprise of your life."

Carlos doubted that. He felt that he had already

had just about all the surprises possible for one life. He didn't believe in any iron horse, but he would wait and see.

The stagecoach was exciting at first. But soon Carlos decided it was not nearly as much fun as their wagon had been. You had to sit cramped in one small spot, with other people around you. You couldn't jump out and trot alongside, picking up pretty stones and splashing through streams and trying to catch little animals. However, the coach did roll faster, and that was something. Carlos liked to hear its driver crack a long whip and shout "HYAH-HYAH-H-H-H, GIT ON, THAR!"

Carlos practiced the shout, and amused the people who heard him. The driver grinned and let him ride outside on the seat that was high above the ground.

"Mighty fine boy you done 'dopted, Mister Gentilé," the driver said at a rest station. "He's polite and smart."

"No sir," the boy corrected. "I am Carlos Montezuma."

He wondered why all the others laughed. He heard Father answer the driver, sounding very proud. "He is ahead of most white boys his age. Why, he learned English in just a few days. Speaks it almost as well as I do."

"And you've been to college. Lucky, having you to learn him."

"I do what I can. I want him to become a doctor, so I must arrange a good schooling."

"Shore, shore thing. A sawbones, hey? Mighty fine work, and we need more of 'em."

Soon they rolled into another city. Here they took

their baggage from the stagecoach and went to stand on a wooden floor without a roof, beside a little house. Carlos wondered about it all, his plump brown face shining with interest.

"This is the station, son," Father told him. "The depot, where the train stops. See that sign up there? It says 'Trinidad, Colorado.' This is the end of the great Santa Fe line, which we'll ride to the East."

Carlos made no answer, partly because several other grown people were staring and smiling at him, and partly because he was confused. He had expected to ride on an iron horse. Now Father said they'd ride a thing called a Santa Fe or a Colorado. Well, he'd just wait. That was always safest.

The boy didn't have to wait long, and when the event did happen it was almost as frightening as the massacre back in Arizona, where he was captured by the Pimas.

Suddenly, they all heard a sound — *whoot whoo-oo-oo-oot whoot!*

That startled him, so Carlos leaned over the edge of the plank floor to look. There, in the distance, he saw a cloud of black smoke, and then he heard another whoot-whooting and a distant rumbling like thunder.

A memory began to come back. Weeks ago, Father had said the Iron Horse would make a whoot-whoot-choo-choo noise and breathe fire. Well, so it did! For there, around the edge of some buildings, came the creature itself! It couldn't be anything else!

The thing seemed to be plunging right at them, and Carlos suddenly turned to flee for safety. But Father was tightly holding his hand.

"Don't be afraid, son!" he shouted, over the great

chuffing and steaming, and the loud dinging of a bell.

The Horse rolled closer — *chuff-chuff, clank-clank, ding-ding-ding, hiss-hiss, chuff-chuff, screeeee-e-e-e-eee clank, PSSS-S-S-s-s-s-sssssssss, CLANK!*

"HEY-O, ever'body!" a man yelled. "Bo-o-o-oard!"

Carlos had shut his eyes. He felt himself hugged close to Father's stomach, and he heard people laughing and talking. People were acting like it was a happy time, in spite of all that horrifying noise. Finally he forced himself to peek.

They stood within a few yards of the Thing. The Horse.

It was long and high and black, and it had huge wheels. The Horse was on fire, breathing it exactly as Father had promised. He heard the fire roaring, saw the smoke and steam rise and saw red-hot coals fall under the Horse.

Carlos felt himself being led down the plank floor. He half shut his eyes again and wished he could close his ears, too, because the noise was so great. The wagon trail, the forests, and plains had never been noisy. That had been a world of beauty and peace. Even worse was the awful smell here. It wasn't just smoke; it was made up of stale grease and soot and dust and sweat and manure from horses and goodness knows what else.

He peeked out to find his way up some steps, Father firmly guiding him by holding a hand. Next thing he knew he was in another wagon seat, only this one was much bigger and softer than any other one he had known. Soon he felt strange, jerky motions, and heard worse noise than ever. His eyes were squeezed tight against it all.

When he opened them, he saw the world whizzing by a window.

"Did — did it — did it eat us?" he murmured.

Father's arm was tight around his shoulder.

"Eat us?" Father squeezed him tighter. "No son, nothing ate us. We're on the train. I don't blame you for being scared. But there's no danger."

Carlos thought about that. His mind was full of other questions, but for the moment, he asked only one more. "Does it burn live horses? So it can have strength to pull us?"

"No!" Mr. Gentilé laughed heartily. "I will try to explain."

The explaining took a long while, and the boy said little though he was very interested. A day and a night had to pass before Carlos began to feel really at ease on the iron horse. He never did quite come to like it, for the thing was too noisy, too jerky, too dirty and smelly, and too crowded with people who stared and laughed at him.

Finally, after what seemed like months, they got off the Horse. Carlos then felt a great sadness. Nobody had said anything, but in his heart he knew that this had been a turning point in his life. He would now have to live in a completely new world.

CHAPTER 10

New Magic

The new world he had entered, Carlos soon discovered, was not as friendly as the simpler one he had left behind him.

He stood on a dirty sidewalk in a city, thinking back to the long happy days in the wagon. Then, he had needed only his beloved Father, the horses, the wild birds, the chipmunks, the squirrels, the rabbits, and the deer for companions. These had been friends enough and he longed to see them again.

"There are more white people here than there are stars in the sky!" he told himself there on the sidewalk.

That was true in the first white city he and Father visited. And it was even more true in the next city. They constantly poured out of doors and crowded the sidewalks. They clattered up the streets in surreys, buggies, and wagons, always making a great noise. They dressed quite differently from the people in far-off Arizona. And while he could understand many of their words, these lacked the soft, pleasing quality of Father's speech.

Nevertheless, he felt a constant excitement, too. The white world held many other children, so plainly there'd be a place for him. And if this was his new world, he told himself, he wanted to know all about it. "If I am going to live here," he told himself often, "I want to know everything the white people do."

So, as the first days in the first city passed, and other cities followed, he asked questions without end. And he received patient answers.

"I am amazed at the way you learn things, son," Mr. Gentilé said to him one afternoon, months after they had left Arizona. "Do you ever forget anything?"

"No sir, I guess not."

"You were born with a very quick mind."

Carlos doubted that. It seemed to him that his mind was being crowded with things too fast! Gone were the easy, relaxed days of riding behind the bobbing heads of old Kit and Blue. Now they ate in restaurants, slept in hotels, rode in swift horse cars on city streets, and saw great buildings that towered to the sky. Everywhere was a clatter of horses hoofs on dirty streets. When Carlos and Mr. Gentilé arrived in the big city of Grand Rapids, Michigan, the smell of the city overpowered him. It had just rained, and in the dampness the odor from the manure on the streets seemed to rise up and envelop everybody. In Chicago, the smell was even worse.

"Everything here seems so very dirty," said Carlos. "Didn't you say that dirt makes sickness, Father?"

"Yes, that is true. When you become a doctor, you will understand why cleanliness is so important."

Two adventures came to Carlos in the huge city of Chicago. The first began on a Sunday morning. That day, Father took him — dressed in fancier clothes than any he had ever worn before — to a church and introduced him to a meeting of other boys and girls.

"Here, people study Jesus' life and his teachings," said Mr. Gentilé.

"Will they teach me here to become a doctor? You have said that Jesus was the Great Healer."

"They will teach you about faith. But to be a medical doctor you must first go to school."

"Who is School?"

"It is not a 'who', it is a meeting. This one is a *Sunday* School, where you learn of God. In weekday school you learn of many, many other things."

The second adventure came as a terrible shock. Carlos and Father had been boarding at the home of a white woman named Mrs. Davis, when one day Father announced that he was going away on a business trip.

"You will stay here and attend school," Father smiled kindly.

"You mean — *stay here without you?*"

It was a horrifying thought. Carlos hadn't been separated from his white father for more than an hour at a time since the man paid thirty silver dollars for the frightened little boy.

He felt a tightening in his breast, and then for a moment his very mind seemed to go numb. He said nothing when the white woman put her arm around him and tried to comfort him. When Father asked questions, he could only stare up at the man in reply, his eyes wide with the horror. At supper that night he said and ate very little. His world seemed to be tumbling down.

Two days later, when his father finally left him there in Chicago, Carlos Montezuma put on a stony face to bid him good-bye. Then the boy went into his bedroom and sat almost motionless for a long hour.

He wanted very much to cry, but crying had been a rare experience in his life. Usually it came only when he had fallen hard and hurt himself. He remembered that in the Apache camp, children hadn't been allowed to cry. If a baby or child began to cry, a mother would clap her hand over his mouth, and would hold it there until the child became quiet. The noise, the Apache mother explained, might attract enemies, especially at night. Wassaja had understood the danger.

But now, in the white world, Carlos was suffering a pain that was deep inside him and was so intense that crying seemed to be the only release. The pain was a powerful longing, and it was mixed with fear. To control his sobbing, he clamped his jaws tight and held a hand firmly over his own mouth. This was all that he knew to do.

Carlos was trying to control his sadness when the white woman came into his room. She had never seen a child behave in this way, and for a time she only stood looking at him in surprise, while the boy stared back with his huge brown eyes. Presently, the woman seemed to understand something of his suffering.

"There, there," she said gently, sitting beside him on his bed. "You mustn't worry, Carlos. I need you here with me, for I am alone too, and I don't have a little boy of my own."

Soon she was holding his head against her, and he found that the pain inside him began to lessen. She petted him, swaying a little. He caught her sweet, delicate scent, and began to relax. She was humming softly now, still patting his shouder and holding him close. It was a new experience, and he liked it.

"I know," she spoke with sudden new enthusiasm,

setting him up straight again and smiling happily. "I'll read to you. Would you like that?"

Carlos didn't answer, for he didn't understand her.

"Wait here. I'll get something to read."

She brought a box of white skins like some he had seen before. The minister who had given him his new name held such a box. His father had one, and there had been one in the place called Sunday School. These had been plain black boxes, and he had not been much interested even when he saw these men seeming to talk to them, though he had wondered about it.

But the box of skins Mrs. Davis brought was very different. It was a light blue, and on the top of it was a picture much like those Father made. He stared at it in her hands. She opened it to one of the thin skins, and it too had a picture on it, and in pretty colors!

"Can you read this page, Carlos?"

He looked at it, then up at her face, saying nothing. She began to look a little surprised.

Putting her finger under one picture, the woman said, "Girl. Let's spell it — g-i-r-l." The finger moved to another picture. "Boy — b-o-y." It kept moving. Dog — d-o-g; man — m-a-n; horse — h-o-r-s-e. Can you spell any of them?"

Carlos's eyes had widened with wonder, but still he said nothing. He looked up at her again, sensing something mighty important here. She had pointed to a picture of a horse, and even though it was a hollow one with only the lines of its body showing, she had said "horse." The same was true of the other pictures.

The woman didn't ask him more questions. She only said, "Let's read a story, shall we? Watch the words as I read."

It wasn't the story itself that impressed him, for Carlos didn't fully understand it. In fact the story as such didn't seem to matter at all. But what did matter was that Mrs. Davis hadn't simply told him the story, she had *said it from the box!* Here was a brand new kind of magic. Why, these boxes could actually capture and store words!

When the woman had finished, he took the book from her hands, slowly opened it, and began to touch the skins. No, they felt smooth, as skins should. The words she got from them had no feeling. Many a time, Carlos had scratched in sand, or had cut marks on smooth trees or boards, and these always felt rough to his fingers. But these magic words were as flat and lifeless as the pictures that Father made!

"It is because you are a woman," he finally said to her, smiling at the answers he had found to his own questions. "It is white *woman's* magic, something white men do not have. Isn't it so?"

Now it was her turn to look startled and confused. She did not reply at once, so Carlos went on.

"Or is it your magic alone? Have you bought me from my father? Did you pay him thirty silver dollars? Do you own me now?"

It was days before Carlos got full answers to all those questions, and they did not come from Mrs. Davis. She had only hugged him to her again as she began gently crying. He made no protest at this, for it was a good feeling to be loved.

Next morning, she scrubbed Carlos, dressed him as for the Sunday School, and took him to a building.

There a sight met his eyes that he had never seen before — dozens, *hundreds,* of boys and girls, running,

shouting, laughing, and playing in one big grassy field.
He and Mrs. Davis stood on the steps of the building
for a moment to watch them. Then another woman
came out.

"I have a new pupil for you," Mrs. Davis told her.

They talked quite a while, but Carlos didn't listen
because the children out there were far more interesting. Then suddenly — clang, clang, clang, clang — a
big bell, louder than the bell on the Iron Horse and
with a deeper tone, rang out over the area. It seemed
to stop everything the children were doing, for they
all dropped their play and ran to the building. They
came at him, Carlos felt, like a herd of animals. He
looked up at Mrs. Davis, but both she and the other
white woman only smiled. The herd thundered up the
steps and on inside without so much as seeing him.
They all were dressed in bright colors, and were laughing and seeming to be happy as birds.

"Now we'll go inside too," the strange woman said,
and took Carlos's hand.

They went into a big room already crowded with
boys and girls about his size. No one else was brown,
but a few were black. He stared at them, and the
laughing and talking stopped. Everyone seemed very
quiet, and everyone stared directly back at him.

"Children," the strange woman said, smiling, "this
is a new pupil. His name is Carlos Montezuma. He is
an Apache Indian. Carlos came from far-away Arizona, but now he lives here. Isn't that nice?"

They all answered "Yes!" in a chorus. But Carlos
Montezuma wasn't at all sure it would be nice. In
fact, he wasn't sure of anything. He was tremendously
excited by what he was seeing but as he stared into

the room, he was growing a little afraid. Each of the children sat at a little table, and on each table was one of those boxes of skins that by some strange magic could capture and hold human words!

CHAPTER 11

Books and
Other Discoveries

The boxes of skins, he learned, also had a name. It sounded much like the voice of a long-legged, long-tailed, long-billed bird that lived back on the Arizona desert, the one called road runner. That funny creature, which he remembered chasing in the fields around the Apache camp, had seemed practically unafraid of human beings. It would glare and fuss at you if you disturbed it. And it would go book, book, book-book-book-book-book! very rapidly.

Now here was the same sound — book. Strange that a bird call and a box of skins with marks and pictures on them would have the same name!

Carlos was fascinated by the little marks in Book. The teacher guided him patiently. "Horse — h-o-r-s-e," she spoke slowly, pointing to each letter with a pencil.

He would smile for he instantly had a mental picture of beloved Kit and Blue, then one of the horses on city streets. And when he saw and heard "l-a-d-y," he thought of Mrs. Davis.

The lessons continued day by day, and by the end of the first week he could read not just words, but also whole sentences. He seemed to remember every detail, every letter and mark. "The lady rides the horse," he read, and he understood now that this could mean any lady, any horse.

In three weeks, Carlos's teacher told him that he could read as well as anyone in the class. This pleased him tremendously. He went home from school glowing inside. By then he was not only reading the strange marks in Book — named Letters and Words — but he was also actually making those marks himself, with Pencil, and even with Pen. Pen was not as easy to handle as Pencil, for Pen required dipping in black water named Ink. If Ink dripped on your clothing or fingers, it stayed there, which made the teacher angry.

After four weeks of school, Carlos's teacher came happily to Mrs. Davis and said, "Carlos has left the rest of the class behind, and must be put in a higher grade. He has the most brilliant mind I have ever taught."

Carlos was not sure he understood what his teacher meant, but he put in a word for himself. "I have to study hard and have a good mind. I am going to be a doctor. Father says doctors must know many, many things. They heal sick people. We had doctors back in the Indian village, but they were not the same." He was silent for a moment as he tried to recall, his black eyes staring off. "They were medicine men," he finally said. "But their medicine — it was not the same. They danced and chanted. There was nothing to take in the mouth. The Sun God . . . and Earth . . ."

He shrugged, and gave up trying to tell of it. His memory had faded, because he had been small back there and so much had happened since he left. The present held such a constant stream of new things that Carlos gave little thought to the past.

After only a few weeks in the school, Carlos realized that he could remember almost everything. It took him longer to understand the strange markings called numbers, but soon he learned to scratch out sums and goes-intos and remainders with the best of them. He felt proud.

"You use up a slate pencil quicker than any other pupil," his teacher told him, smiling. "You are working at something all the time, Carlos."

"I like school," said he, and meant it.

Four other boys overheard that remark, and they spread the news of it on the playground. When Carlos came out at end of the day, they were waiting. One, the largest, had been chosen to do the teasing.

Carlos saw the big one approach him while the others watched. He didn't know what to expect, but he felt a flash of warning, an instinct that spelled danger. It was as if he and Father had suddenly come onto a mountain lion in the wilderness of Arizona. His muscles tensed, his eyes glared straight into those of the taller grinning boy.

"I like school!" The big boy pretended to imitate Carlos, speaking in a high, girlish voice. Then he changed to a deep, threatening tone. "Well, see here, Injun, if you think—"

He got no further. Carlos, surprising even himself, knew to get in the first blow. He swung his fist like a lightning bolt. The older boy fell backward and rolled. Then he sat up and looked at Carlos in astonishment.

"Gee whillikers!" some other lad in the group murmured.

Without a word, Carlos Montezuma walked on. Never again was he teased by schoolmates, though he remained very watchful. He knew that an Indian was as good as a white boy, and was prepared to fight about it.

Every hour in school brought discoveries. He quickly learned that he could draw pictures of houses, horses, wagons, birds, and trees. Sometimes he sketched Miss Marshall, his teacher, and worried because his pictures were not as clear as Father's photographs of people. He thought perhaps that the magic of the camera must come from Jesus. Father seemed to be a very close friend of Jesus.

He found that the world was round, and this interested him for days. He made a world of clay, and scratched continents on it with Miss Marshall's help. He tried counting the stars, too, but gave up after he reached two thousand.

Gradually, too, Carlos realized that he was interested in girls. He hadn't thought much before about how different they were from boys, but now he began to take notice. "They are much like boys only they have long hair and wear dresses," he wrote in a letter to Father. "They are like women, but boys are more like horses and dogs."

He said as much to Miss Marshall, too, and wondered why she laughed. "That's very interesting, Carlos," the teacher added.

One day, quite unexpectedly, Mrs. Davis told Carlos that Father would return in the afternoon.

"HOO-RAY Yeow-YEOW!"

His outburst startled both the lady and himself, and he felt a little ashamed. From somewhere deep inside him had come part of an old Apache yell of excitement and pleasure, and it seemed strange to him now.

But it was not long before he was excitedly chattering to Mrs. Davis about Father's return from his business trip.

That afternoon, Carlos dressed in his best clothes, and he was smiling broadly when Father stepped off what the boy now knew to be named Train. At first they shook hands, rather formally, Mr. Gentilé bowing a little and Carlos bowing slightly in turn.

Next moment they leaped together in a great father-son bear hug. The man lifted Carlos and whirled around with him, laughing and patting his son on the back, while strangers looked on and smiled. The boy sensed that this must not be a usual sight — a white-skinned man hugging a dark-skinned boy. Naturally, onlookers would be curious.

The two rode home in Mrs. Davis's surrey. The city horse, named Molly, pulled it with a proud *clop-clop-clop* against the cobblestoned streets. Carlos asked to drive and he found that Molly seemed to have more life than plodding old Kit and Blue. Once she reached over to nip the neck of a gelding whose buggy had pulled alongside hers, and the gelding obediently dropped back. Yes, mares were bossy.

"Mares make the male horses mind them," Carlos said.

Mr. Gentilé smiled broadly. "That is sometimes true in the world of human beings also, my son."

Father and Mrs. Davis laughed, and Carlos wondered what was funny. He did not quite understand how horses and people were alike. Father saw his questioning look, and spoke up again.

"Time enough yet to learn about women, son. About girls. How have you been doing in school?"

Mrs. Davis answered for him. "Excellent! Miss Marshall says he is the leader of the class."

Carlos slapped Molly with the reins. "I want to be a doctor, sir."

Mr. Gentilé nodded. "The field of medicine is a good opportunity for helping other people. But what of your arithmetic? Do you still count on your fingers and toes, eh?" He smiled, and Carlos knew that he was teasing.

"I can say the whole mul — multican — mul —"

"Multiplication table?"

"Yes sir! Two t'ms one is two; two t'ms two is four; two t'ms three is six; two t'ms —"

"Hold on, hold on!" The grownups laughed gently again. "We will hear it all later. But we are proud of you, son."

Mr. Gentilé reached into his pocket and took out a leather pouch. The top was bound in metal, with two little knobs in the center that snapped around each other. He twisted them open, reached into the pouch, and took out a shining silver dollar.

"Here, fellow. I am proud of you. You may spend this dollar when you find something special that you want."

Carlos thanked him, gripping the dollar hard. But he finally put it in his pants pocket, for he needed both hands free to handle Molly's reins.

Next day he took the dollar to school and showed it to everyone. The other boys envied him. Only a few had ever actually seen a whole dollar, much less owned one. They stared silently at it and at him. Carlos felt that they saw him as "different," but that they respected him, too. It was not an unhappy feeling.

CHAPTER 12

Growing Up

Time passed.

He did not actually measure it, but he saw the sun constantly changing its path through the sky. He also watched the moon choose new locations. Every Indian boy learned to look for such things at a very early age, he recalled. The knowledge of time's passing was soon taken for granted.

Even so, the seasons slipped by him. They became years before he realized it. Sometimes he wished that he had written down his many adventures. Many white girls, and some white boys, kept diaries. In them they wrote something almost every day. He spoke of them once to his father.

"It is something like an old man in the Pima village where I was held captive," the boy recalled. "I mean, his recording things. He made notches on a long stick. Every sixth day he would sit in front of his hut and cut on it. Sometimes he carved little designs, not just notches. I think *he* was marking the days and weeks as they went by."

Mr. Gentilé nodded. "Yes, he was, son. I have heard about that. The old Pima was the tribal Time Man. He was carving a calendar stick. And he was recording a history, too. The old man not only counted the weeks, months, and years on his stick, but he also noted special events. We can be sure that he cut a record of the Pimas' raid on your Apache village. Later he probably carved something about your being taken prisoner and sold to me."

Now that was something! He, Wassaja, was in history! It would be something to tell about in school.

Carlos had not lived long in the white man's world before he decided that Christmas was his favorite time of the year. The word *Christmas* had confused him when he first heard it from Mr. Gentilé, but he soon knew all about the colorful season — its lights and gifts and parties, and its deeper meaning as well. One year, on December 26, Carlos told Father that he wished he could bring Christmas to the Apaches and all the other Indians.

"Yes," agreed Father. "So do I. Perhaps, when you are grown—"

No more was said about it, because a group of young people arrived at the house just then. They had come to invite Carlos Montezuma to a party.

It was a girl — a very pretty one — who spoke for them. Carlos usually avoided girls, for he was very shy. But this one, popping out of the group laughing and talking, seemed to have him cornered.

"Monte!" she cried. "You are coming to the party with us! You *have* to!" She laughed with eyes and mouth together. "We drew straws. I am your date!"

He looked at her in surprise. She had not called him Carlos, but Monte! A nickname. That meant acceptance. He was no longer a kind of outsider because of his dark Indian skin. Monte! He smiled back.

"Will you, Monte? All right?"

Not only had he a nickname now, but he also had a girl friend!

His mind began racing. Father had often said that he would "like" girls some day. Had the time come? He had seen and spoken to girls here in the white world. Sometimes he had even played games with them in school. But generally he saw girls as people apart, quite different from boys. They *were* different, his mind told him again. But the difference seemed, all at once, to be in their favor.

He laughed, somewhat self-consciously, and said to this one, "All right, I'll be glad to come to the party."

There was more cheerful talk among the young people. Carlos enjoyed it, even though he spent most of the time listening. Later, he asked Father what he should say to people, especially to the girls.

"Do I speak with them just as I would with boys?" he asked

Mr. Gentilé, a bachelor, admitted that he was not an authority on how to talk with girls. But he tried to help. "I should say, son, just treat them with extra courtesy. I believe it best to let them take the lead in the — ah — social amenities."

"Sir?" Carlos didn't understand.

"What I mean is, just let matters take their natural course. Girls seem to have more social grace than boys have, at this age. She will probably guide you, without your knowing it."

Carlos truly hoped so. He didn't want to appear awkward, or ill-mannered, or too shy. He was shy, he knew, but he didn't want it to show. If the girl would really do most of the talking, everything might be all right.

A crowd of some fifty young people gathered in the church that evening, and as it happened, the girl did exactly as Carlos had hoped. Early in the evening, he lost her for a short while. Then he heard her suddenly call him.

"Monte!" It was almost a shriek, but she had used his new nickname, and he appreciated that. "Monte, you must be the first."

He saw her beaming face as she ran up and asked him to play the part of a reindeer in a game that the group had started. It seemed that he was to be the lead deer on a sleigh team, pulling Santa Claus. So, they hitched him up with a red ribbon harness. The girl put a set of pasteboard antlers on him. She stood back, admired him, and said, "Now!"

Sure enough, Carlos began snorting and pawing and acting as he imagined a reindeer might act, as he leaped across the Christmas sky at midnight. He lost any self-conscious feeling. He heard the laughter, the merry play, and began having a truly grand time.

When the party had quieted down some, the pretty girl spoke again. "Monte, tell us about life on the Indian lands, won't you? We are very interested."

He heard a chorus of encouragement, and the others quickly made a circle there on the floor. All sat looking at him. Carlos had become used to this request, though, for he had been asked many different times to tell of his boyhood.

So he grinned and said, "All right, I'll tell you about it. But remember, I was only a little kid then."

He told whatever came to mind. He explained about

trapping rabbits and birds, about the wickiup homes, about his parents and sisters. He told of the ritual dances, and the warfare.

Then questions came in a quick chorus, and they all talked a long time. There seemed to be a lot of questions, and he knew only some of the answers. No, he did not agree that all Indians were cruel. Yes, he thought they could learn to be friends of the white people. Yes, he thought they could learn the white people's language.

"Talk some of the Indian language to us," a boy suggested.

"I'm afraid there is no such thing as 'the Indian language.' There are as many different Indian languages as there are tribes. I am Apache, but I did not understand a word that my captors, the Pima Indians, spoke. Nor would I understand, say, the Sioux, or the Cheyennes."

When the party broke up and Carlos went home, he sensed his friends had a new respect for him. In some ways it was almost an open admiration. "You are the smartest boy in church, Monte," the girl told him. "But I already knew that. The pastor says you are precocious."

He didn't really understand so he just smiled, thanked her, and wished everyone good night.

At home he shyly asked Mrs. Davis what "precocious" meant. She said that a precocious person is one who is very mature for his natural age.

He tried to think that out. If he really was precocious, he decided, it was because he knew about Indians, in addition to knowing about white people. Also, God had sent him an educated white father, and

Mr. Gentilé had taught him many, many things.

"But it doesn't mean that I can get a big head," he warned himself. Nevertheless, he was pleased to be precocious, especially if the girl thought it a good thing to be.

Life in the white man's world was very good, but as Father had warned him long ago, it wasn't all perfect. One day, he was insulted by someone he didn't even know. He had stopped at a little restaurant and ordered a ham sandwich.

The restaurant man scowled and said, "I don't sell to niggers."

Carlos was so astonished that his mouth dropped open, and he stared at the rude man. Finally he spoke. "I am not a Negro. But even if I were, what has that got to do with . . . ?"

The man interrupted. "What are you, then?"

"I am an Apache Indian."

The man held out the sandwich. Carlos took it, paid for it, and went away thinking about the incident. He had seen many Negroes, and had known some Negro children well. His own skin was darker than that of some of them. He felt tremendously confused, for he was not used to such prejudice and could not understand it.

But he was too interested in life to be set back by this experience. Every day, almost every hour, brought surprises and excitements.

One day, Father came home with a new surprise. Carlos, working over school books, looked up to see bright excitement in the man's eyes.

"We are leaving!" Mr. Gentilé said with no warning. "We are moving to New York City!"

Carlos jumped up. "New York? Father, that's the biggest city of all!"

"Exactly, my son. I think we will both do better there. I will open a photograph studio. You will go to school. New York is the seat of American culture, and you will learn many things there."

CHAPTER 13

More
School

The move to New York City proved to be
a mistake. It was exciting enough to make the long
trip on the train. And Carlos found the huge city itself
a place of great interest. But for the second time in
his life, Carlos Montezuma, now called Monte by all
of his friends, felt that he had been torn away from
home.

"Of course, this change is not as big as the one I
made when the Pimas captured me," he wrote back to
Mrs. Davis in Chicago. "Even so, it has made me feel
mighty sad. It's not that I really dislike New York.
The city is huge and beautiful, though it is somehow
frightening, too. But it is not a western city as Chicago
is. The people even speak differently. Father is not as
happy here as he was in Chicago, either."

Mrs. Davis wrote back, trying to encourage him.
"You will be all right as soon as you make new friends.
Try to meet some nice girls as well as young men.
They will think you are very handsome, as I do."

He already knew that he was considered handsome.
The girls in his new school made that fact clear at
once, and he was pleased. He was only in his early
teens, but he was already a big, strong fellow with a

full, strong face, not an awkward youth like many in his age group. Carlos gave one of Father's photographs of him to a girl he met at a Sunday School party. But when the boys started teasing him about that, he stopped seeing the girl.

"Monte, you should be on the stage," a new friend told him one day. "Why, you could play a brave."

He ignored that idea. In stage plays, the "Indian brave" was nearly always a very unreal character, who did not act or speak like a real Indian. Carlos felt that, though Indians might not have white skin, they were people, too, with human feelings and needs, just like whites. It was simply that so few of them had the chance to get an education, such as he had. He himself had been given that chance, and had proved that he could learn as well as any white person.

But in spite of this, the New York people would not accept him as their equal. They were either scornful of him or they were amused by his appearance. Carlos realized that Mr. Gentilé had seen their attitude, too, and he soon knew that Father was not happy in New York, either.

One night over their supper, Father said, "Perhaps we should not have come here, my son. We do make money in the photograph studio here, more than we need. But I liked Chicago better, and I think you did too. As a matter of fact, I enjoyed traveling in our wagon with Kit and Blue best of all. Do you remember?" The good man smiled.

"Do I! Oh Father, yes! Could we buy a new wagon and team and do it again? Go back on the road? We could load up your camera and things, and take pictures as you used to do. I could help you now. I could develop them for you, even take them myself. You could live an easy life. I would drive and feed the team and cook the —" Carlos's mind was racing, and his heart was pleading.

Father, still smiling gently, held up a hand. "You do tempt me, son. But you must stay in school. I will not have you grow up to be an old wanderer, such as I."

"Father, that's silly! You are the best-educated man I know."

"But *you* won't be educated if you become a road tramp again. You need classical training."

"Now what does that mean?"

Mr. Gentilé was patient. "It means knowledge from great books, taught by skilled men and women. This knowledge is beyond photography and the first years in school." Here, Mr. Gentilé looked sharply at Carlos, and pointed at him with a dessert fork. "Though I will say this for photography, son. The time will come when it is recognized as an art, just as painting and sculpture are. Mark my words."

"It already is, sir. To me."

"But not to most people. They just see it as something new and unusual, the people all standing stiff and sour faced, and the prints never very clear. Why, Carlos, I venture to say that the time will come when man will be making photographs in *color!* Color, mind you, that is not merely painted with brushes, but is the same as nature has put into our world. But then, maybe that's only a dream," he said sadly.

Finishing his meal and wiping his lips, Father added, "No, you must go on to school here."

"Yes sir," Carlos nodded soberly.

In this way, the father and son convinced themselves that they should stay in New York. Then suddenly, a change was forced upon them.

It was about two o'clock one morning and Carlos was sound asleep. New York was always noisy. Any hour, night or day, the sound of hoofs on pavement, the rattle of iron-tired wheels, and the call of drivers made a distant roar outside the windows and doors. But on this night, the noise was different. The boy rubbed his eyes as he sat up in bed. His mind began to focus on the sound of shouting outside.

Somebody was banging on their front door and yelling, "HEY, MR. GENTILE! GET UP, GET UP! YOUR STUDIO IS ON FIRE!"

Carlos threw off the covers and leaped to his feet. In a moment he had on enough clothing to run outside. Then he found that the shouted words were all too true, for Father's studio was covered with flames. The very sight of the fire sickened him, as his mind flashed back to the night of the massacre long ago in Arizona.

A crowd had gathered, but it was too late to do anything. They could only watch while the building and its contents burned. Shortly after daybreak, father and son sadly returned home. The man's arm was around the boy's shoulder.

"Nobody was hurt," Father said, quietly. "We have that to be thankful for."

They had re-entered their home before the boy spoke again.

"Father, perhaps now would be the time for us to go back westward again. I still want to. Do you?"

Mr. Gentilé nodded. Carlos could see sadness in the man's dark eyes, and had then to control his own emotions. He felt a great sympathy for his father.

So, the year 1878 saw them again in the growing city of Chicago. Carlos had agreed that they shouldn't try to live in a wagon again; times had changed and their needs were different. They would try to set up a new business in the big city. Father found some friends and borrowed money from them, then Carlos walked the streets with him until they found an empty store. Father ordered a new camera, new supplies, and furniture for the studio.

Together they painted a neat sign and nailed it across the front of their new studio. They also had some advertisements printed on sheets of paper. Carlos carried these to homes and businesses up and down the streets for many blocks around. The advertisements read:

For permanent photographs

B O U L E V A R D E   S T U D I O

3907 Cottage Grove Avenue

Chicago

Near the junction of Oakwood and

Drexel Boulevards

Large Photographs by a Patented Process

A Specialty

Horses and Carriages Photographed

Formerly 103 State Street

Carlos Gentilé

Carlos thought that advertisement looked very fine and dignified. Moreover, he saw that it brought in business. One day Father allowed him to take his first big photograph for a customer. It was a beautiful lady sitting in the seat of a buggy, holding the reins of a beautiful horse.

"Make us look grand," she said.

"Yes ma'am," Monte replied, and smiled.

He ducked under the big black cloth that covered the camera. There he focused the upside-down image of the horse, buggy, and lady on the ground glass at the back of the camera. Then he came out, made a few more preparations, and grasped a bulb at the end of a long rubber tube. He looked up.

The lady was sitting stiff with her head back, and she now looked quite severe. The horse was rubbing its nose on its knee. When it stopped rubbing, its head still hung low.

"You are prettier than that, ma'am," Carlos said. "Would you please smile big? . . . There! Much better."

But the horse had gone to sleep.

"WHEEE-E-EIST!" Carlos gave a short sharp whistle.

The horse's head went high, and its ears stood erect. *Click-snap.*

Next week he delivered the picture, and it delighted the woman. Carlos got a fat fee of two dollars for it. Mr. Gentilé was so pleased that he allowed the boy to keep it all.

This event took place shortly after the day that he and Father had set up as his fourteenth birthday. Of course, they could not know, for sure, exactly when he had been born. But everybody needed a birth date. So, with the help of a white doctor, Mr. Gentilé and Carlos had made a close guess. Lately, he often said, he could almost feel himself grow. He looked much older than fourteen. But the growth still wasn't fast enough to satisfy him. Carlos was eager to be grown, for he had big plans.

Carlos soon was taking pictures almost as skillfully as his father. And he saw that his father was tempted to train Carlos as his assistant.

"You *could* stay with me and learn this business," the man thought aloud one day. "But no, I say! Photography gets in the blood. You should study medicine."

"Yes sir."

"So it's school for you. As much as I can afford."

Carlos was not unhappy with the thought, although at times he did have questions about what he wanted to do. "Sometimes," he told a friend, "I want to be a lawyer. Or a storekeeper. Or a rancher." But what Carlos thought about most often was being a doctor. He told his friend, "Perhaps in time I could bring the white man's medicine to my own people."

Most people who heard Carlos's plan thought this was a fine idea. But one boy didn't see it that way. "Why should you want to do that?" he asked. "The only good Injun is a dead Injun. They scalp and kill and steal and —"

"I am an Indian."

The white boy paused a moment, then added, "That's different."

"Why?"

"Well, well shucks, it just is. They — they're there, you're here. You don't have to go nurse them."

Carlos left the other boy, feeling confused and angry.

About a month later came a real shock. One day Carlos learned by accident that his father was not prospering. The boy had gone into Father's studio after school to help out. He was quietly at work in

the darkroom when he overheard Father talking with
a man out front. Monte knew the man's voice. It was
that of a Baptist minister, the Reverend W. H. Steadman, who lived nearby in Urbana, Illinois. Carlos did
not know how the two had met, but he knew they had
become friends.

"The fire in New York broke me," Father was saying. "I had to borrow money to set up the new studio
here. I am gradually paying it back, but I have too
little to keep the boy going. He is brilliant, Mr. Steadman. He needs the best schooling a boy can have."

Carlos was dismayed, but he began thinking right
away. Should he quit school? He could get many jobs
and earn his own way. His mind was filled with these
thoughts when he heard the minister speak.

"My friend," said Rev. Steadman, "you have a done
a fine thing in taking this Indian boy and rearing him."

"It was a selfish pleasure, sir. I wanted a son."

"You wanted a son, but it was not selfish of you.
And you have done a remarkable job. Carlos is far
beyond his age in education and general knowledge.
He speaks and acts like a grown young man. So if
you are facing a financial shortage, would you trust
my wife and me? Would you let young Carlos come
and live with us until you can get on your feet again?
Would you let him stay with us and continue his
schooling?"

Carlos could contain himself no longer. He stepped
through the door and around the curtain into the front
waiting room.

"I have been listening," said he simply, his face
very grave. "I didn't mean to, but I couldn't help it. I
heard your offer, Mr. Steadman."

The two men were very surprised, and they only stared at him, until finally Mr. Gentilé spoke.

"Facts have to be faced," the man said. "I am very sorry and very embarrassed, my son. And yet, perhaps this is an act of God. You are indeed growing up, and I may have given you all that I have to give. New opportunities have to be grasped when they arise."

Carlos forced a big smile. "Stop worrying. I want to go to school, and Mr. Steadman is providing a way. It's as simple as that. When do we leave, Mr. Steadman?"

He had made it easier for his father, but it wasn't easy on himself. The very idea of leaving Father was depressing.

So it was, then, that Carlos Montezuma entered a wholly new kind of life. While he was preparing to leave, he did a lot of thinking, and realized that many changes lay ahead.

For one thing, there was a Mrs. Steadman. Would she be like the landladies and women teachers he had known? They had all been gentle and kind. Would Mrs. Steadman be the same?

Carlos ceased to worry when he met Mrs. Steadman. She spoke softly and smiled at him with loving eyes, and asked him to call her Mother. It was a word that hadn't had much meaning in his life. But now the term began to come alive for him, and he wrote his father that the growth of it in his consciousness was like discovering a beautiful new flower.

Even so, his time with the Steadmans was much too short. The two had barely become acquainted with one another when yet another sudden and important change came. Carlos had been in the public schools of Urbana, only a few weeks when Mr. Steadman came home one afternoon beaming with pleasure.

"Monte," he called, "good news!"

The boy hurried from his room where he had been doing homework.

"What is it? Is my father coming?"

"No, not that. But see here — you are going to college! Immediately!"

Carlos showed his astonishment. "College? . . . *Me?* . . . But I'm only fifteen years old!"

"No matter." Mr. Steadman beamed happily. "I was talking with the principal and some of the teachers in your school and with some of the leaders in our Young Men's Christian Association. We discussed you at length, Monte."

"But why? What about? I mean, what did —?" He paused, confused.

"We went over your school records. Mr. Gentilé has taught you many special things, and you are far ahead of the average boy your age."

"But I have no money."

"That's where the Young Men's Christian Association comes in. They will see to it that you get a chance, and later when you are earning money, you can pay back your debt. It amounts to a loan. They want you to start immediately in one of the finest colleges of all, the University of Illinois. I accepted for you."

They talked out the details, and gradually Carlos realized that boyhood was over. "From now on," he told himself earnestly, "I must talk and act like an adult."

That evening, Carlos walked alone outside. Leaning on a fence, he looked up at the stars, thinking. They were beautiful, as always; he did not often see them so bright, here in Illinois. Perhaps this brilliance tonight was a good omen, a promise of success.

He wondered if Cocuyevah and Thilgeya, his Apache father and mother, might be up there among those stars. Heaven was supposed to be up there somewhere. Perhaps they could see him here on earth, and would even help him to be happy and strong in the white men's world.

CHAPTER 14

The Great Plan

Life in college, Carlos soon discovered, was very different from anything he had known before.

"I thought I understood what the word *school* meant," he wrote Mr. Steadman one day. "But this is not at all like elementary or high school. The studies here are much harder. The professors seem to expect a great deal of us."

But Carlos really had no fear about his grades. Somehow, to his delight, he had always been able to learn things fast and to remember what he learned.

"It is because you know how to concentrate," one instructor told him. "Most young freshmen do not know how, and their minds jump around in every direction."

The thought surprised Carlos, and it interested him too. As he began to think back over the years, he decided that his Apache father, Cocuyevah, had started that kind of skill in him. He could even recall certain words that Cocuyevah had spoken: *Pay strict attention to whatever you are doing. Train your eyes and mind to see everything and remember it. Your life may depend on that.*

Because of his quick mind, his interest in his studies,

and his excellent health, Carlos went through college with ease. His grades were always excellent. In 1884, Carlos was graduated *cum laude* (with honor), with a Bachelor of Science degree in chemistry. He graduated at nineteen, an age when most boys and girls were just entering college, and his graduation came *barely thirteen years after he had seen his first white man!*

Again with the help of the Y.M.C.A., Carlos went right on into medical school. It was here that he discovered what he called his Second New World.

The first one, of course, had been that of the white people. His dramatic jump into the white world had been an exciting experience, one filled with discovery. Why, even his first piece of candy was exciting! He well remembered. It had been like a stick from a tree, was somewhat longer than his fingers, and was white with red stripes. And of course those first photographs, and the iron horse, and so many other things.

And yet, all of those wonders now seemed small, compared to his newest discovery. For here, in medical school, he actually began exploring inside the human body!

"I remember that we Apache children thought of the body as a kind of mystery," said Carlos. "We put things in at the top, and fewer of them came out, in a different form, at the bottom. Nobody seemed to understand why. I remember I had the feeling that a Great Spirit lived inside my mother's body, and possibly my father's as well. Sometimes I wondered if maybe I didn't have a small Great Spirit inside my own body somewhere, and I would try to talk to it. Perhaps it was a small Sun God. Or maybe an Eagle

God. The feeling was very vague, yet very strong. The body, with its blood which we often saw, was a tremendous mystery."

As a small boy in the Arizona wilderness, Carlos had known about death, too. He had seen many animals die; indeed he had killed many himself. He also had known that human bodies die, although when this occurred, the Apaches had hurried to make the body of the dead person "go away." As a very small child, he never learned just *how* it was made to go away. The person who had died, from whatever cause, simply disappeared. Nobody explained to him why this happened.

Carlos had never looked at the inside of a human body, beyond seeing the inside of his mouth. In fact, he had never thought of doing so. Thus, medical school was something of a shock. Not only must he look inside a dead person, but he must also spend much time studying the body.

"Every detail of muscle and bone, sinew and cell, must be understood by you who would become doctors," the first professor told his class.

When the first dead body — called a cadaver — was actually opened in his presence, Carlos felt a chill of fear leap through him. But of course nothing happened. No Sun God leaped out. No Eagle God took wing. It was all very quiet and casual. The instructor lectured, and he showed the class certain muscles and other things that needed to be understood.

Carlos went to his room that night feeling as though he had somehow been hypnotized. He wasn't exactly afraid, but he was filled with wonder. He hadn't realized that a doctor actually had to learn all about the "innards" of human beings, in order to doctor them.

For a long while, Carlos dropped all his social contacts and did nothing but study. He slept too little, because his mind was fascinated with so many important facts. He ate too little. He played not at all. Finding the valve that controlled the human heart and the blood flow was more important than playing baseball or skating. Locating the opening from the stomach into the intestines, and tracing the swallowed food as it passed all the way through a human being — *these* activities held him.

As a boy, Carlos had always quietly assumed that the human body was hollow. You swallowed food as if you were dropping it into a basket. Somehow, it bounced around in there and went through what white people called "digestion." But exactly how, he had no idea.

Now he learned that food went into a place called the stomach. And much illness began right there! "I have decided to give most of my study to the stomach," he wrote Mr. Steadman. "The stomach feeds the brain, and everything else, or at least starts the process of feeding. When people get sick, I have noticed that most of the time it seems to begin in the stomach. Sometimes they eat the wrong things, I believe. Or something goes wrong with their digestion. I keep wondering why.

"There are theories, Mr. Steadman, that little animals live in foods. They are so small we can't see them. But in the stomach they are likely to multiply and make the human being sick. Could this be true, do you think?

"Many doctors draw blood from sick people. 'Bleeding them,' it is called. Just open a vein and draw out a lot of blood. To me, this does not make sense. If blood is dangerous, why did God put it in there? I think the sickness starts not in the blood but in the stomach. That is usually where the pain starts, isn't it? Yes! I have had stomach pains myself. Maybe certain foods — unclean foods, perhaps — cause those pains. I intend to find out. Perhaps as a doctor I can do some good work."

Mr. Steadman wrote a letter of encouragement. And Carlos continued to work very hard in the laboratories, and in his room, studying. Within a few years, he was graduated from medical school with very high marks, adding to his name an M.D. — Doctor of Medicine — degree.

CHAPTER 15

"Medicine Man"

During his last two years in medical school, Carlos Montezuma had begun to be concerned about more than just medicine. He had been looking ahead, for he knew that he would graduate soon, and would need to set up a practice as a physician. But where would he start?

His thoughts had turned back to his own people, the Indians. He knew that the Indians of America were still very isolated. Most still lived in a state of near poverty, and they had not been treated fairly by many white men. "I want to help my people," he told his friends.

Carlos's first move, out of medical school, was to offer his services as a physician to the Indians. Almost at once, this got him a job on an Indian reservation in North Dakota.

When he got there, he was shocked. All of the doctoring was still based on superstition. Many American Indians here and elsewhere died for lack of proper food and medical attention. Carlos was deeply saddened by this knowledge. "I must try to be a real medicine man for the people."

But Carlos soon discovered that the Indians did

not want him to doctor them. They did not trust white remedies, and preferred their own medicine men. Carlos did some work in North Dakota, but very little. He was depressed and dismayed, and he eventually left there.

Brooding about his failure, he returned to Chicago and tried to form a new plan for serving people. Perhaps, he told himself, if he could learn first to doctor white people, he could then start again to help his own kinsmen.

Good fortune came his way in Chicago. He happened to meet an elderly doctor who was a stomach specialist, Dr. Fenton Turck.

"Ah yes, Montezuma," the old one said. "I know about you. An Indian, who made top grades in medical school. A stomach man, as I am. Good personality, too. Tell you what. You come into partnership with me. Then I will gradually turn over my big practice to you and I can retire. I need to, for I am getting along! What do you say?"

Young Carlos was astounded.

"Sir, I would like nothing more. But would the white people of Chicago want a doctor who has a brown-red skin, an Apache Indian?"

Dr. Turck scoffed at that. "What of that? American, aren't you? Talented, and honest, too."

The two physicians, old and young, talked the matter out for an hour. In the end, Carlos joined Dr. Turck as invited. And within a few months, the young man had taken over all the older man's practice.

His color did not shock the Chicago people, as Carlos had feared. In fact, it seemed to add to his appeal in that he was something of a novelty. And his manner was impressive, without being conceited. People trusted him.

Soon Carlos was so busy that he was working day and night. At almost any hour, the people of Chicago might hear his horse and buggy rushing him to the home of a sick person. He became known to hundreds of folks and as he rode up the street they would wave and speak to him. He always returned their greeting with a lift of his buggy whip, a nod of his head, and a bright smile.

Many of Carlos's patients were foreign-born and could not speak the English language very well, if at all. Other patients were very wealthy, though he also worked with sick people who had little or no money. He never sent a bill to any of these poorer folks, but many came to his office voluntarily, to pay what they could afford. Very often while visiting a home, Carlos would observe that a family of poor patients hadn't enough food. Within a few hours, then, a grocery wagon would deliver boxes of food to that home, and the grocer would not tell who sent it. But the people soon learned! Many thought of Carlos as a saint.

While he was working in Chicago, Carlos belonged to many organizations — such as a singing society, and the organization of men known as the Masons, who devoted much time to helping mankind by doing unselfish good works. Carlos said that the Masons' ideals fitted in exactly with the ideals that Mr. Gentilé had given him.

But in spite of all his activity, he was lonely at times. "A man needs a wife," he once said to friends in the Baptist church he now attended. "Perhaps I should go to Arizona and find an Apache girl."

Sometime later, a beautiful woman came into Carlos's office. She was about his own age. "My name is Maria Keller," said she. "I am Hungarian, and I do not know many people in Chicago. But I have heard that you might be able to help me, for I have a bad stomach pain."

Carlos treated her pain, and cured it. And he also fell in love.

This experience was entirely new to the young doctor. He felt that he was walking on clouds! He went around his own home singing, and he bought himself new clothes, and flowers to send to Maria Keller.

"I am acting silly!" he told a close friend who laughed at him.

"For heaven's sake, go court the girl!"

Dr. Montezuma thereupon took himself in hand. And for the next few weeks his buggy, with its rubber tires going *ss-s-s-sss* behind the rhythmic *clop-clop-clop* of his horse was heard and seen carrying him and pretty Maria along the streets of Chicago. The big doctor was always beaming with pleasure.

Many friends attended their quiet wedding and gifts poured in from dozens of people he didn't even know or remember. Carlos had entered his third New World, and he was happier than ever before.

When the pair returned from their honeymoon, Carlos plunged into work again. And he found that Maria had ideals as high as his own. She helped with the patients; she helped with the charity work; she helped to save money. Maria, he told everyone, was truly a miracle sent by God.

CHAPTER 16

Going
Back

One night, a few years after his marriage, Carlos came home and spoke to his wife in a very serious manner. "Maria," said he, "I feel it's time to make a change in our lives."

Maria sensed that he was deep in thought, and she waited a few moments before speaking softly, "Change our lives, Carlos? How?"

He moved across the room to stand at a window. He seemed to be looking far away. Again she waited.

"For the better, I hope. I owe a debt, and I must pay it."

She went to a rocking chair and sat down quietly, folding her hands in her lap. "A debt? But I keep your record books and I know nothing of any debt, Carlos."

With his back to her, he smiled gently. He moved behind the window curtain and stared out at the night sky, hands clasped behind his back, thinking. When he did not answer her, Maria began again.

"The truth is, Carlos, we are wealthy. You have become the society doctor of Chicago. You do much charity work, but the rich people also use your services, as you well know. And we have saved our money; we have more than enough."

He turned and came back through the curtain. "That's just it! That is why I must make a change."

"I don't understand."

"No. I'm not even sure that I do, myself. It is something inside me. Something very strong; something that I must do. It is not a money debt, Maria, it is a — a heart debt, I suppose we should call it. To Carlos Gentilé, for his faith in me. And perhaps through him, a debt to God. Maria, beloved, I feel that I must now go back to my own people."

He spoke with such earnestness that she was impressed. Her next words were barely above a whisper. "You want to go back to the Apaches?"

"Yes! My kinsmen. My own tribe. As you know, I have visited the Apache reservation a few times since I became a doctor. I saw the poor conditions there — the ignorance, the poverty. My people are worse off than when I was born! They have become dependents of the white government. Instead of having pride to hunt and make their own living, they sit around and wait for the government Indian Bureau to feed and clothe them. They have been forced into the white men's world, but they haven't been given the opportunity to succeed in this new world. I want to help them through education. I can travel all over America, lecturing and writing about the poor condition of the Indians. I will try to help all tribes, but I will start with the Apaches because I know them best."

Maria was looking up at him, her eyes wide.

He went on. "The Indians have become America's forgotten people. I believe I can help them get back their dignity. They will live in equality with the whites. Will you work with me, Maria?"

A smile lighted her lovely face. "Of course, my Carlos."

"Then we must start planning at once. I must give up my practice of medicine, and find a younger man to take over. First I will go directly to Arizona and talk to my people, so that they will understand. Then I will campaign across the nation to win white support. My people are now weak. They must be able to become strong and free. I see my own life as proof that they can do so!"

There was fire in Carlos's manner now. But he quieted down under Maria's gentle encouragement, and together they talked for hours. They made many plans, many promises to themselves.

It was near midnight when their talk ended. Carlos asked Maria to go on to bed, saying he wanted to think for a while longer. He kissed her goodnight, and then walked slowly to their front door, opened it, and stepped out. Chicago was silent now. No house or street lights could be seen, but the black velvet sky was gemmed with stars, and a sliver of moon had joined them. Carlos had always felt a special kinship with the moon. He often thought of it as a night eye that was placed by God to watch over man. Even now, though the eye was partly closed, enough of it was open to be on guard.

As he looked up into the night sky, Carlos placed his strong forearms on the top of the fence around his yard. He was quiet for a moment, and then he whispered, "Thilgeya, Cocuyevah, I know you are up there somewhere with the beautiful stars, you and my sisters. You will know what I now plan to do for our people. Guide me and help me if you can."

Epilog

Carlos Montezuma did indeed devote his final years to helping his fellow Indians. As he had expected, he did not meet with instant success. He was often misunderstood, by whites and Indians alike. But he made so much progress, became so well known across the country, that President Theodore Roosevelt offered him a position as Director of the United States Indian Bureau. Carlos refused the honor, saying that he could best serve his people as a common man, not as a head of an organization in Washington.

He developed a list of Indian reforms that were very much needed. He exposed ways in which dishonest white men were stealing from the Indians. He set up plans for helping Indian tribes to improve their farming, cattle raising, and mining. He helped develop a system for more efficient tribal governments, and showed how they could set aside money for any lean years that might come. But most of all, he worked for better health and living standards.

Dr. Carlos Montezuma, a distinguished American Indian who lived most of his life in the white men's world, and was beloved by thousands for his kindness and unselfishness, died in Arizona on January 31, 1923.

His wife Maria died several years later in Chicago, and was buried in that city. The couple had no children. After Carlos's death, he was laid to rest at Fort McDowell, not far from the region where he had been born and had lived as a small boy. This was the way he wanted it.

And what became of the family of the Apache boy Wassaja?

You will remember that the lad saw a Pima arrow pierce his father's body on that night of the massacre. It is known that Cocuyevah died right there.

Wassaja's two sisters were taken prisoner by the Pimas. Later they were sold, for a milking cow, to a white family who took them to Mexico. Both girls died there shortly afterward.

The mother, Thilgeyah, escaped the massacre and made her way to an army post, where she was kept as a prisoner. But she yearned for her little son, and one day she escaped her guards and started out alone to search for him. She could not know, of course, that he was in good hands.

Two Indian policemen, hired by the white army, saw her leave and mistakenly thought she might bring back Indian warriors for an attack. They called out to her to halt. Probably she did not understand, for she did not obey them.

The policemen raised their guns and fired, and Thilgeya, the mother of Wassaja, died there on the side of the mountain.

Finally, what of Carlos Gentilé, the kindly photographer?

Almost all that is known of him is told in the story here. You will remember that he sent the boy Carlos to live with the Rev. Steadman in Urbana, Illinois. After that, Mr. Gentilé is largely lost to history.

We can assume that he went back to Chicago and worked in his new Boulevarde Studio. In time he must have prospered, for it is known that his portrait hung for years in the Chicago Press Club.

Mr. Gentilé died in Chicago in 1893, and was buried there in Mount Hope Cemetery. Carlos Montezuma had long since begun his life as a healer of men, and Mr. Gentilé died proud of his Apache son.

Carlos Gentilé, as photographed in 1883

Dr. Carlos Montezuma, as photographed in 1915

THE AUTHOR

Adele Arnold is a native of Texas, and a graduate of Rice University in Houston. She and her husband, a fellow student, settled in Phoenix, Arizona, and there became fascinated with Indian legend and lore. The couple built a large Indian style pueblo home of native adobe, and it was featured in three magazines as a significant contribution to American architecture. For some years Mrs. Arnold taught in Phoenix elementary schools, and has published two books on aspects of teaching mentally retarded children.

Mrs. Arnold is the wife of the distinguished author, Oren Arnold. They have three daughters, and eight grandchildren. The family still lives in Phoenix during the winter, and they have a summer home in California near the blue Pacific.